MC

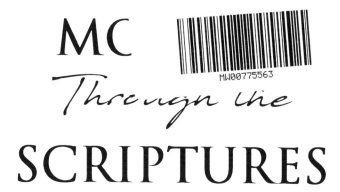

Through the

SCRIPTURES

Of Them That Danced

MOVING
Through the
SCRIPTURES

Of Them That Danced

REKESHA PITTMAN

Moving Through the Scriptures:
Of them That Danced

Copyright © 2020 by Rekesha Pittman.

All Scripture quotations, unless otherwise indicated, are taken from the King James Bible Version.

ISBN: 978-1-7342508-2-4

Editor: The Treasure Team

Cover Design: USEntarprise

Printed in the United States of America.

Get Write Publishing
14850 Montfort Drive – Suite 290
Dallas, TX, 75254

TABLE OF CONTENTS

ACKNOWLEDGEMENTS

To my Lord and Savior, by Whose Spirit I have been given this revelation…

To every dancer that has allowed me to pour into their lives in an hour, a season, or over the years…

To the many apostles, prophets, pastors, evangelists, and teachers who have pushed, propelled, and encouraged me to submit to the calling of God on my life…

To the reader, for desiring a more excellent ministry through the study, love, and willful obedience of the Word…

I give God thanks for you.

"If you have a heartbeat,

you have rhythm."

– Rekesha Pittman

INTRODUCTION

Teaching about the ministry of movement over the years has been a blessing, a privilege, and a challenge. For at least the past two decades, information has increased in the dance ministry realm and more dancers are seeking to study the Word of God and its stance regarding movement.

Along with the joys of teaching, I am also perplexed by the great number of those who dance both inside and outside of the church, yet possess very little information about the subject. Dance classes, worship arts conferences, public festivals, workshops, seminars, online resources, webinars, professional Christian dance companies, mentoring programs, and specialized services have multiplied by leaps and bounds. In spite of an enormous pool of available resources, the masses still remain largely undereducated about the passion so many of us proclaim.

For those who have applied fundamental biblical knowledge and have experienced the miraculous, we are rejoicing together. Even with the increasing amount of information available, there is yet more for us to discover regarding this divine opportunity to communicate the Gospel through the language of dance.

Many are familiar with David and Miriam as principal dancers in the Bible. Unfortunately for far too many, the familiarity of dance ministry history ends there. It is time to take additional steps to get a broader understanding and remove any limitations we may have imposed through our own "dance ministry rulebooks."

Where the Spirit of the Lord is, there is liberty! I pray that you receive this message with an open heart, ready to receive all that the Spirit of the Lord desires to reveal. Let's move beyond the mundane and stretch far beyond our own borders as true disciples of the Word in its entirety.

Chapter 1

MOVERS

When I ask dancers about the first time that
dance is mentioned in the Bible specifically,
many refer to Miriam in Exodus 15:20,
while others refer to Genesis 1:2. Exodus
15:20 is the first time **dance** is mentioned in
the Scriptures, while Genesis 1:2 is the first
time **movement** is introduced. We will
discuss Miriam in detail in a later chapter.
First, we will take a look at the birth of a
movement unlike any other!

> *"And the earth was without form, and
> void; and darkness was upon the face
> of the deep. And the Spirit of God
> <u>moved</u> upon the face of the waters."*
> – Genesis 1:2

The Hebrew word for the "Mover"
(Spirit) used here is **ruwach** (Strong's
#7307), meaning *wind, breath, mind, spirit.*
The One doing the moving is the Holy
Spirit. Note that the Spirit of God moved

3

over the face of the waters. As the earth was formless and empty, we can assume that there was an absence of movement prior to that period.

If there was no movement before the Spirit appeared over the waters, they had to be motionless. Anyone taking a glance into still water knows that a reflection results from being face-to-face with it—similar to looking into a mirror. I can only wonder what revelation came by the Spirit that produced movement! The Spirit of God provides illumination. Immediately after this moving encounter, God said, "Let there be light: and there was light." (Genesis 1:3) Oh, the Glory of His Presence!

The meaning of moved in the original Hebrew for Genesis 1:2 is **racaph** (Strong's #7363) meaning *to brood, flutter, move, shake.* It would be correct to say that this was the first time that movement was mentioned in the Bible. He is the First, the Alpha, and the Beginning. How appropriate for those of us created in His image to move according to His example!

A general reading through the Scriptures reveals a text saturated with movement and moving symbolism that paint a clear picture of His Living Word. It is almost as if intricate choreography is captured within the pages of black and white (and sometimes red), to give us a foundation of how important movement is for helping us to better understand the nature of both God and mankind. The simple stretching of the hands, placement of the feet, walking, running, kneeling, extensions, and clapping are but a few of the descriptive movements recorded.

Classifying what we do as merely "dance ministry," "praise dance," "liturgical dance," "worship dance," "mime," and many other modern dance styles may serve as an injustice. Broadening this genre into "the ministry of movement" embraces many expressions of physicality that includes both the trained and untrained disciple alike.

New movements and dances are still being birthed. We must avoid the tradition of forcing a movement discipline into just one or a few narrow categories. Whenever the Spirit was present in the Scriptures, supernatural, inexplicable things occurred!

Many dancers use a popular quote from the New Testament in the book of Acts as a mantra:

"For in him we live, and <u>move</u>, and have our being; as certain also of your own poets have said, for we are also his offspring."

– Acts 17:28

Kineo (Strong's #2795) is the Greek word used here, meaning *to move, set in motion, to move to and fro; a riot, disturbance, to throw into a commotion.* In this definition, we find generic imagery as well as some problematic elements. Movement can be both positive and negative. The power of movement is that it can set things in motion as well as cause unrest and disturbances in an atmosphere.

Many dance ministries have experienced intense praise and worship encounters after a particularly effective piece that shifted the mindsets of people and sparked a revolution simultaneously. We must use movement with precision that causes us to succeed with God's strategy each and every time. When we do, only then are we truly moving in the miraculous.

The root word for kineo is **kio**, meaning *to stir*. Another familiar word that means movement in Greek is **kinesis** (Strong's #2796) which means *a stirring; moving*. Movement is an essential sign of life. Although most of our actions are not choreographic in nature, normal daily activities like walking, talking, sleeping, etc. are all inherently rhythmic in nature. The very center of our physical existence is based on an internal organ that keeps time: the **heart**. No doubt about it—we all have rhythm!

A focused and concentrated study of movement throughout the Scriptures must administer a dose of reality. All dance in the Bible is not necessarily done in honor or praise unto God. We cannot assume that all dances in the church are done for His glory either.

Just because something is written in the Bible does not automatically give us permission to include it in our praise and worship offerings. What if He instructs us to move a different way? If the visual presentation is anointed, it will destroy yokes no matter what dance style is presented. We must seek the Lord's direction for each piece that appears before Him and His people.

The ministry of movement can be categorized in multiple ways. Some terminology is popular, while others are still developing via ever-changing, newly-emerging creativity and the passage of time. Let's not be guilty of confining dance to our own traditions or mandating that only formal training styles be accepted as legitimate.

COMMON CATEGORIES OF MOVEMENT IN THE CHURCH

Praise Dance
Liturgical Dance
Worship Dance
Prophetic Dance
Sacred Dance
Interpretive Dance
Hebraic Dance
Flag Ministry
Banner Carriers
Standard Bearers
Pageantry
Mime
Gospel Hip-Hop

COMMON MOVEMENT DISCIPLINES

African Dance
Ballet
Modern Dance
Contemporary
Folk Dance
Jazz
Hip-Hop
Latin Dance
Mime
Sign Language
Tap Dance

While some dancers or groups may classify themselves as one genre or discipline, many are beginning to incorporate elements of various styles for broader vocabulary and greater visual communication. The use of creative garments, colors, flags, banners, props, lighting, screens, and other visual aids have greatly enhanced the storytelling aspect of the movement minister today.

Many current Christian dance productions rival professional shows and costumes of modern times. Multiple entrepreneurs and businesses that cater to this niche market are growing and becoming increasingly lucrative. As dancers of the faith embrace education, technique, and ongoing training, the investment into the ministry of movement will continue to increase and spread on an international level.

The next several chapters of this book will provide revelatory, in-depth study of all the defined dancers of the Bible: good, bad, and otherwise. Even in the moments of infamy in the Word, we may still take valuable notes that will help us become more effective today. Let us begin to move through the Scriptures!

Chapter 2

MIRIAM

Students of Christian dance are largely familiar with this woman who danced with a timbrel in her hand. If there was a "Hall of Fame" for dancers in the Bible, Miriam would probably have been inducted into it. Biblical studies will identify this instance of dance in Exodus 15:20 as "The Law of First Mention," which documents the first time this exact word was used in the Bible. It provides a basis from which further studies can be compared and contrasted. The Scriptural account is as such:

> **"And Miriam the prophetess, the sister of Aaron, took a timbrel in her hand; and all the women went out after her with timbrels and with dances."**
> — Exodus 15:20

From this account, we can gather several significant details. Miriam was a prophetess, which meant she had a voice that was used by God to communicate with His people. In addition, she was a female in a position of public leadership. Being the sister of Aaron also confirms her as the sister of Moses, the famed leader of the Israelite people who led them out of the bondage of slavery under Egyptian rule. Miriam placed an instrument in her hand—a timbrel, which was routinely used to accompany song and dance in the Bible.

An often-overlooked detail in Exodus 15:20 is that **all** of the women followed Miriam with timbrels and dances (and not a small number of them!). They were not just passive observers, but active participants in the dance. In modern times, this would designate Miriam as the official dance ministry leader. Using dances in the plural form would also suggest that there was more than one dance being presented or more than one type of dance happening simultaneously.

Further study of Exodus 15 reveals a larger backdrop from which to learn about the significance of this dance. The beginning of Exodus Chapter 15 resounds with a song:

"Then sang Moses and the children of Israel this song unto the LORD, and spake, saying, I will sing unto the LORD, for he hath triumphed gloriously: the horse and his rider hath he thrown into the sea."

— Exodus 15:1

"And Miriam answered them, Sing ye to the LORD, for he hath triumphed gloriously; the horse and his rider hath he thrown into the sea."

— Exodus 15:21

Here we witness a type of the "call and response" tradition during which the song went forth from Moses and the children of Israel and the response to the song was agreement through dancing and singing by the larger community of women.

Throughout many of the Old Testament Scriptures, we find that lyrical singing, dancing, and musical instrumentation are often closely linked. Many dancers in the church today have followed this same pattern by dancing to pre-recorded songs (lyrics and instruments) and moving in conjunction with live praise and worship teams (singers, musicians, and dancers) during regular church services and on special programs.

As biblical tradition would dictate, men returning from victorious battle would often be greeted with songs and dances given by women of ancient times. This trend of continuity can also be seen at male sporting events via cheerleaders and dancers that encourage them with song and dance. In this case, Pharoah's army was drowned in the midst of the Red Sea as the surrounding waters defeated both men and their horses in death. Post-battle celebration ensued, as was customary and expected.

Students of biblical dance must take a deeper look at Miriam and extract valuable lessons regarding her life and leadership to get a more complete understanding. It may be a surprise to many that Miriam's name is derived from the Hebrew word **Miryam** (Strong's #4813), meaning *rebelliously*. The root word for Miryam in Hebrew is **meriy** (Strong's #4805), which means bitterness. Although Miriam is frequently celebrated by dancers for being a heroine of Biblical dance, we must also take note of the need to stay humble before the Lord, or we too may find ourselves ensnared by rebellion.

In Numbers Chapter 12, Miriam and Aaron verbally criticized Moses regarding his marriage to an Ethiopian woman. As a prophetess, Miriam confidently asserted that the Lord spoke to her as well as Moses. The Lord Himself responded to the dispute and clearly distinguished that He spoke to Moses face-to-face and not in visions, dreams, or dark sayings (like He spoke to the traditional prophets).

As a result of her lack of reverence for Moses, Miriam became leprous. Moses, her brother and spiritual leader, interceded for her healing. Although God answered the request, Miriam still had to remain separated from the people for seven days after her affliction.

Dancers in the church arena who are not careful can become guilty of operating out of rebellion. Those serving in positions of leadership must exercise special caution. Miriam's sin was impactful for multiple reasons. As a leader of influence, her outspoken criticism of Moses could have resulted in division and discord among the people. Because she was a prophetess, God provided revelation through Miriam as He still does with many prophets today. Those in the ministry of movement must realize that even though God may impart a specific message to deliver, it is not always appropriate or timely to leap into operation.

Many dancers can fall into the trap of rebellion through the root of bitterness. This may stem from hurtful experiences with church leaders, conflicts with fellow ministry members, unresolved family issues, personal struggles, or a lack of understanding of God's Word. Some groups are formed out of perceived rejection or lack of acceptance by leadership. Although many ministries outside of the local church congregation may be ordained by God, special care must be taken to establish ministries in righteousness and not rebellion. Waiting for the Lord's revelation is always better than running ahead of His instruction.

Accepting a position of leadership must not be taken lightly. Dance leaders who misuse their God-given influence can easily fall into sin and cause others to be affected by the error. Miriam's public punishment hindered the progress of the children of Israel for seven whole days! It is no doubt that this also affected her credibility as a leader in the eyes of the people, considering that lepers were outcasts in the community as unclean beings. Although Moses' cry to God granted her healing, Miriam still had to suffer the penalty for openly challenging the Man of God.

Not all dancers are leaders by title, but standing before a group of people makes all who stand in front of them, in essence, leaders. Many disagreements and a lack of unity can be traced to petty complaints, idle talk, malicious gossip, and the feeling of co-equality with leaders that some exhibit today. The concept of leadership has been somewhat diminished due to public scandals and broken trust on behalf of leaders in both the local church assembly and the larger Christian community.

Like Moses, leaders must have a close relationship with God and be called by Him for the assignment. Like Miriam, those who misuse their positions will ultimately pay the price for their rebellious behavior. Although Miriam's death was recorded in Numbers Chapter 20, a sobering reminder was given to the children of Israel in the Book of Deuteronomy:

"Remember what the LORD thy God did unto Miriam by the way, after that ye were come forth out of Egypt."
— Deuteronomy 24:9

Although Miriam's example was the first time that **dance** was mentioned expressly by name, it does not necessarily indicate that it was the first instance of dancing being done historically. It is written in Exodus 15:20 that all of the women followed after Miriam with timbrels and with dances. Unlike many instances of movement that we experience in the church today, we see dance in the Bible as a communal activity and a normal part of life.

In the custom of folk dance of Biblical times, men and women danced separately.[1] Since we are aware that thousands upon thousands of people were present at the crossing of the Red Sea, we can only imagine how many women danced with Miriam! In order to dance in a safe and organized fashion of any kind, we can also conclude

---

[1] https://www.myjewishlearning.com/article/jewish-dance/

that there were certain steps that had to be learned in advance or followed in order to keep step in the process.

Acknowledging that dance is first mentioned because of the efforts of Miriam, let's take a closer look at the instrument she used to further study the history and traditions of Biblical dance. Remember how we reviewed the origin of movement in the opening verses of Genesis? This was covered in the previous chapter. We also find another interesting artifact in Genesis as well:

"Wherefore didst thou flee away secretly, and steal away from me; and didst not tell me, that I might have sent thee away with mirth, and with songs, <u>with tabret</u>, and with harp?"
– Genesis 31:27

According to Strong's #8596, the specific Hebrew word used here is **toph**, meaning a tambourine, tabret, or timbrel! This would count as the first mention of tabrets (or timbrels) in the Scriptures. The origin of the word timbrel comes from the Hebrew word **taphar** (Strong's #8609) meaning to sew, or women that sew together. Further defined regarding its usage is **taphaph** (Strong's #8608), a Hebrew word meaning *to drum, play as on the tambourine: taber, play with timbrels.* According to Gesenius' Lexicon, "A timbrel is a drum beaten in the East by women when dancing; it is made with a wooden circle, covered with a membrane and furnished by brass bells."

Notice in Genesis 31 that songs and mirth (gladness with laughter), were listed along with the timbrel. In this context, Laban is speaking to Jacob who left with his wives (Laban's daughters) without his foreknowledge. Laban is implying that he would have sent Jacob off with a celebration that might have very well included dances with timbrels. Although we cannot cite this as an instance of dance by name, the use of timbrels with music and celebration was common in Old Testament times.

The use of the timbrel and tabret were common in the Bible. They were utilized for dance, during prophecy, with other instruments, and in battle. Let's examine several passages that highlight this instrument and its importance:

"After that thou shalt come to the hill of God, where is the garrison of the Philistines: and it shall come to pass, when thou art come thither to the city, that thou shalt meet a company of prophets coming down from the high place with a psaltery, and <u>a tabret,</u> and a pipe, and a harp, before them; and they shall prophesy: And the Spirit of the LORD will come upon thee, and thou shalt prophesy with them, and shalt be turned into another man."

– 1 Samuel 10:5-6

This account happened shortly after Saul was anointed by Samuel, before he was installed as king. In this case, Samuel told Saul that he would meet a group of prophets utilizing various instruments along his journey, of which included the tabret. Here we observe prophecy being used in conjunction with music.

In Christian dance, there is a growing number of "prophetic dancers" that use music along with movement and, at times, audible words to prophesy and deliver a message directly from God. This is usually conducted in the presence of a congregation.

Later in 1 Samuel, we see the tabret used with song, dance, and instruments:

"And it came to pass as they came, when David was returned from the slaughter of the Philistine, that the women came out of all cities of Israel, <u>singing and dancing</u>, to meet king Saul, <u>with tabrets</u>, with joy, <u>and with instruments of musick</u>."
– 1 Samuel 18:6

With Miriam's example, as well as the tradition of women coming out to greet the returning victor from battle, we can picture multitudes of women going forth in the dance, intermingling song with musical instrumentation. Not only did these women dance, they were singers and musicians as well!

From this emerged another reaction known to accompany the dance: **envy.** King Saul was ruling at the time and David was serving in Saul's court. Returning from the slaughter of the Philistine, the women came out to greet King Saul (not David, his servant), but sang a song in Saul's presence that made the King look inferior in front of his entourage:

"And the women answered one another as they played, and said, Saul hath slain his thousands, and David his ten thousands. And Saul was very wroth, and the saying displeased him; and he said, They have ascribed unto David ten thousands, and to me they have ascribed but thousands: and what can he have more but the kingdom? And Saul eyed David from that day and forward."

- 1 Samuel 18:7-9

We will discuss more about the community of women that danced as well as David in our later studies, but we can clearly see here the similarity between Miriam and the history of dancers that followed in her footsteps through the incorporation of song, instruments, and dance as a community effort.

Moving forward into 2 Samuel, we read about the tabret as a continued part of the praise celebration:

"And David and all the house of Israel played before the LORD on all manner of instruments made of fir wood, even on harps, and on psalteries, and on

timbrels, and on cornets, and on cymbals."

- 2 Samuel 6:5

David has his heart set on bringing the Ark of the Covenant into the City of David, so he gathered the people together to help him celebrate. A large gathering of musicians were playing instruments, including timbrels. Note that this was the first time David attempted to bring the Ark of God into the city, but he was unsuccessful at doing so because God was not consulted about the proper order.

If we were to take a sneak peek at the second attempt to bring the Ark to the place David had prepared for it, we see that it was now accompanied by the dance of the king (2 Samuel 6:14). Although 2 Samuel 6:5 (David's first effort with the Ark) does not explicitly state that dance accompanied the parade of the Ark, we would probably be surprised if dance was excluded in the first attempt to transport the Ark of the Covenant.

The presence of the tabret did not always indicate that the work of the Lord was in progress:

"And the harp, and the viol, <u>the tabret</u>, and pipe, and wine, are in their feasts: but they regard not the work of the LORD, neither consider the operation of his hands."

-Isaiah 5:12

This was the judgment concerning impurity among the people. As Miriam experienced a time of judgment and the resulting impurity of leprosy, those who take on the form of celebration to the exclusion of the One to be honored will be operating in vain.

Dancers who dedicate themselves to the Lord's service half-heartedly are placing their lives in danger of judgment. This warning is not limited to the novice dancer, but to the veteran as well. Positioning one-self based on titles, experience, and good intentions is not what the Lord uses as qualifiers. Obedience is the order of the day and is required of the Lord. We see this judgment continue in the Book of Isaiah:

"<u>The mirth of tabrets</u> ceaseth, the noise of them that rejoice, the joy of the harp ceaseth."

– Isaiah 24:8

This sentence not only affected the people (as it did with Miriam) but extended to the land as well. Because of the sin of the people, the gladness of the tabrets was absent from the streets, along with its usual accompaniments. For the dancer, this could represent a local church being affected by sin in the dance ministry or congregation that causes the dance to be put on hiatus or removed from church services altogether. Dancers desiring to move according to truth must proceed with caution!

The prophet Nahum describes the victorious armies of God and the penalty that will be paid for those who suffer defeat:

"And Huzzab shall be led away captive, she shall be brought up, and her maids shall lead her as with the voice of doves, <u>tabering</u> upon their breasts."

– Nahum 2:7

Instead of experiencing a joyful song and dance with tambourines, those who oppose the Lord will endure mourning and the absence of celebration. Instead of striking the timbrel with their hands lifted, the beating of the chest in lament awaits those who become enemies of righteousness. Dancers who want to remain in the will of the Lord must be set apart for His service and clearly identified as His people.

Thankfully, the story of the tabret does not end in judgment! The Lord Himself selects it as instrumental in battle:

"And in every place where the grounded staff shall pass, which the LORD shall lay upon him, it shall be <u>with tabrets </u>and harps: and in battles of shaking will he fight with it."
– Isaiah 30:32

Amazingly, the Lord uses a tabret! The verses above this describe a very visual recording of a song accompanied by musical instruments and denotes how the Assyrian would be beaten down through the voice of the Lord.

Keeping with the theme of the returning victor and responding through dance, many Christian dancers employ what is known as "warfare dance" during group gatherings and for personal use. Warfare dance is often very aggressive, strategic, and loud! Often, it is done to upbeat music that includes instruments, percussion, and declarative lyrics.

Even though dancers like Miriam faced challenges along the journey, it is encouraging to know that the Lord is still in the restoration business as we see in the Book of Jeremiah:

> **"Again I will build thee, and thou shalt be built, O virgin of Israel: thou shalt again be adorned <u>with thy tabrets,</u> and shalt go forth in the dances of them that make merry."**
>
> – Jeremiah 31:4

We see the pattern set again, as with Miriam, of tabrets or timbrels and dancing operating in conjunction.

The Word is consistent in its depiction of the use of the timbrel or tabret together with dancing, singing, and other instruments as a public response to victory. This was often a community effort and embraced by vast numbers of women, of whom Miriam is most remembered. As a general reminder of the importance of all of these elements working together, we read in the Book of Psalms that:

> **"The singers went before, the players on instruments followed after; among**

them were the damsels <u>playing with timbrels</u>."

– Psalm 68:25

The Word of God must always take priority—whether it is being demonstrated visually or experienced audibly. For Christian dancers, the mission should never be one that highlights creativity above the Creator. The singers were at the forefront, meaning, the message must be heard to be clear. Following behind the lyrics are the musicians, who must be careful not to overshadow the Word with vigorous playing or magnified volumes that will mask the meaning intended.

If dancers are not mindful, songs may be selected based on a rhythm that is void of solid Biblical backing or Scriptural reference. In the midst of all of this activity, we find our beloved maidens—timbrels in hand—joining in with the singers and musicians in a united effort to accompany the glorious entrance of God and King into the sanctuary.

An awesome display of solidarity is birthed when carrying out God-ordained assignments! Miriam was indeed a prophetess, though she allowed herself to become blinded by pride and rebellion. By the mercy of God and through repentance, Miriam was forgiven and restored to her people. This story gives us precedence, inspiration, correction, and notes the power of repentance and forgiveness as essential for every dancer in the Christian faith.

As a final note, Miriam was sent by God, just as Moses and Aaron were to serve as leaders of the people. Micah 6:4 confirms this:

"For I brought thee up out of the land of Egypt, and redeemed thee out of the house of servants; and I sent before thee Moses, Aaron, and Miriam."

Miriam's position was not confined to the background. She too, was sent to stand before the people of God. How she handled her position was her decision.

It is important to realize that how we stand in front of the people is not to be taken lightly. Miriam heard from God, moved in authority, and also moved out of turn. A commission by God requires a submission to His leadership. Knowing God's

Word will produce more movement. Let's be careful to make sure our words do not cause others to stall or fall.

Chapter 3

THE CHILDREN OF ISRAEL

It may be difficult for us to accept that we can be corrupted. When dance is first mentioned by name in the Scriptures, we see an entire nation of women singing and dancing victoriously before the Lord after passing through the Red Sea. Just a few chapters later, things take an interesting turn…

"And the LORD said unto Moses, Go, get thee down; for thy people, which thou broughtest out of the land of Egypt, have corrupted themselves: They have turned aside quickly out of the way which I commanded them: they have made them a molten calf, and have worshipped it, and have sacrificed thereunto, and said, These be thy gods, O Israel, which brought thee up out of the land of Egypt."

– Exodus 32:7-8

It is important to remain faithful to God. The Lord let Moses know that the people were quick to abandon the instructions that were given. It still pains me to hear time and again how so many movement ministries reject biblical teaching and the training elements of dance and are only interested in learning a routine. The children of Israel wanted to do things according to their own preferences. Many dancers are still doing this today.

Notice that the Lord did not even claim these people for Himself in Exodus Chapter 32! The word for worship in this passage of text (Strong's #7812) is **shachah**, a Hebrew word meaning *to bow down*. They also gave credit to an idol god for delivering them out of bondage. Not only were they establishing their own order for worship, they fully embraced deception to justify what they were doing.

As we continue to dig deeper, we discover that the root word for worship in this passage (Strong's #4284) is **machashabah,** meaning *thought, device, plan, purpose, invention*. Even before this unsanctioned worship became a physical act, there was a thought and plan developed for it in advance. In the absence of their leader, Moses, they were able to seduce Aaron the priest into allowing them to make a golden calf with the gold jewelry they were wearing. Where did these gold baubles come from? They received them when they were leaving Egypt!

"And Aaron said unto them, Break off the golden earrings, which are in the ears of your wives, of your sons, and of your daughters, and bring them unto me. And all the people brake off the golden earrings which were in their ears, and brought them unto Aaron."
– Exodus 32:2-3

The text says they had to **break off** the earrings that were being worn by entire families! They had literally become attached to the ways of Egypt and were willing to exchange their own wealth and the inheritance of the next generations in order to reproduce what they had experienced while under Pharaoh's rule.

The bull was an Egyptian deity[2] and must have been seen by the children of

---

[2] https://www.ancient.eu/Apis/

Israel while they were slaves. How many Christian dancers today still seek to retain the traditions they learned before surrendering their lives to Christ simply because it is familiar? He has a more excellent way for us.

Gesenuis' Lexicon defines **machashabah** (worship) as *that which anyone meditates, purposes, or plots i.e. a counsel, project; often specially of evil counsels. Artificial work.* The children of Israel hatched a plot against themselves as they decided to form their own opinions while Moses, their trusted leader, was spending time getting instructions from the Lord.

It is important to have Godly leaders in place. When people are left to govern themselves without the voice of God, they will be inclined to act on their imaginations. Aaron was left in charge, but Aaron was the one taking orders. In that moment, he pleased the people more than he feared God.

I have heard countless and tragic stories about division within dance ministries. Both leaders and dancers have been sabotaged, abused, mistreated, and misunderstood. The seed of discord often begins with one person or a group of people that grows into an unholy war.

As I began to dig deeper into the problems plaguing dance ministries, I discovered that much of them can be attributed to a lack of understanding by the leadership. Apostles, Pastors, Bishops, Elders, Overseers, and ministry directors have been guilty of implementing activities without biblical accountability. Many senior leaders will openly admit that they have limited understanding regarding the ministry of dance. There are church leaders who have a passion for worship arts that includes dance, but this is often the minority and not the majority.

One of my own challenges as a worship arts educator is to witness the ongoing apathy regarding knowledge of the Word of God for far too many praise/worship/mime dancers. For the purposes of training, many more are interested in the mechanics of "how" to dance, and neglect "why" we dance. As a result, performance has become far more prevalent than power.

Moses understood the importance of spending personal time with God. Although the children of Israel were invited to know God for themselves, they decided collectively to rely on Moses. Later, Moses became so overwhelmed with the people that he was advised by his father-in-law Jethro to appoint 70 assistants!

Today, we all have access to the Father. Neglecting to take personal responsibility for knowing God's instructions as a worship dancer is a very dangerous position. Devising our own interpretation and leaning to our own understanding of what constitutes movement as a ministry will result in failure. God knows what He wants from us and we should give it to Him!

It is challenging to understand how people can witness God perform miracles and wonders but still pursue their own personal definition of worship. Moses came down from the mountain and discovered the following debacle:

"And it came to pass, as soon as he came nigh unto the camp, that he saw the calf, and the dancing: and Moses' anger waxed hot, and he cast the tables out of his hands, and brake them beneath the mount."

– Exodus 32:19

38

The infraction was so great that these reveling dancers forfeited the promise because they insisted on doing things the way they thought best. The tradition of the Egyptians was so ingrained in their hearts that they were convinced it would be acceptable to serve the Almighty God and themselves at the same time. Tragedy ensued.

The irony in Moses throwing and breaking the tablets (or the Ten Commandments) on the golden idol was that the directions God spoke concerning them were as follows:

"Thou shalt have no other gods before me. Thou shalt not make unto thee any graven image, or any likeness of any thing that is in heaven above, or that is in the earth beneath, or that is in the water under the earth. Thou shalt not bow down thyself to them, nor serve them: for I the LORD thy God am a jealous God, visiting the iniquity of the fathers upon the children unto the third and fourth generation of them that hate me."

– Exodus 20:3-5

God's instructions were already broken in their hearts before they were destroyed on the tablets. Though there was a precedent set when Miriam led the dance, it was quickly abandoned as soon as the people saw an occasion to lead themselves.

Leadership is necessary for all of us. Even dancers who are leaders must still walk in humility regarding other servants of God. When there is an abandonment of Godly principles, there will ultimately be unwanted repercussions for disobedience. The Lord's desire is not to punish us, it is to bless us for obeying His will.

This is the problem with adopting the world's practices into Godly worship. The molten calf was carried with them in their hearts from Egypt. Egyptians were noted as a culture and society that served several idol gods, one of which was the bull-calf deity.

The Apis bull was worshipped in Egypt and Mesopotamia.[3] Apis was an Egyptian god of strength and fertility. The Egyptians believed that the spirit of Apis was inside of the body of a real bull that would be kept by Pharoah each year and cared for luxuriously. Pharoah would then consume the flesh of the bull as a way to inherit the power of this

---

[3] https://www.newworldencyclopedia.org/entry/Apis

spirit himself. Every year, a new bull would be located, groomed, and then sacrificed in this annual ritual.

Historically, the Egyptians danced nude in public with a ribbon tied around their waists.[4] Following the pattern, the children of Israel mimicked this practice in Exodus 32:25-26:

> **"And when Moses saw that the people were naked; (for Aaron had made them naked unto their shame among their enemies:) Then Moses stood in the gate of the camp, and said, Who is on the LORD's side? let him come unto me. And all the sons of Levi gathered themselves together unto him."**

I doubt it a is coincidence that the Hebrew word used for *naked* here is **para** (Strong's #6544), which means *to act as a leader, ignore, neglect, to show lack of restraint.* This word is also translated as *uncover, naked,* and *bare.* As leaders, it is important to make sure that the people are not dancing in front of the enemy uncovered.

---

[4] https://www.ancient-egypt-online.com/egyptian-dance.html

In the church community, dancers who minister without appropriate clothing can cause shame to come upon them. This can also include being uncovered in the sense that they do not have on the full armor of God. Allowing dancers to move publicly without salvation is dangerous.

A lack of faith can cause a breach to come into the camp. Living lives void of righteousness encourages sinful lifestyles to be embraced. The inability to handle the truth allows deception to overtake the ministry. Ignorance concerning the Word of God and how it applies to movement will undoubtedly produce rebellious activity in the ranks. Neglecting to maintain peace may cause the ministry to be dismantled entirely.

In the absence of the primary leader (Moses), the children of Israel provided their own counsel and began to pressure Aaron to serve their agenda. In order to submit to the order of God, we must know when we are serving our flesh and when we are abiding in the faith. Aaron's insecurity ultimately placed them in danger.

As a priest, Aaron was trained in the laws of God and was separated to serve Him.

Although he assisted the people in making the golden calf, the Scripture indicates that he also "made them naked to shame them." Here is yet another warning for leaders not to place people in positions to embarrass them openly. Harsh criticism, derogatory comments, unfair discipline, and controlling behavior will result in massive losses to the ministry.

When we consider this scene in contrast with the detailed instructions that Moses was given for adorning Aaron and his sons with priestly garments in Exodus 28, they were to be fully covered. Holy garments were purposed for beauty and for glory, and the worship was both orderly and precise. These vain worshipers were stripped of any connection to the priesthood by wearing nothing at all. Leaders who aim to look better than those who follow them have the wrong motives.

Leaders must be cautioned against setting their followers up for failure. Instead of giving the children of Israel a denial, Aaron taught them a lesson for which they would pay dearly. To make matters worse, Aaron tried to convince Moses that the calf merely appeared out of the fire. Making excuses instead of taking responsibility for leaders will result in damage that may be impossible to repair.

Leadership is a responsibility that brings either victory or defeat. Those who danced did not have to be slaughtered. The error happened within the camp. Aaron's leadership had been compromised and the people paid the ultimate price.

Aaron became an accommodating leader who permitted people to influence him as he led them away from true worship. Church and ministry leaders cannot be more concerned with pleasing the congregation in terms of music preference, dance styles, and worship expressions while neglecting to seek the Lord's direction as to what type of worship pleases Him.

The repercussions were severe. An angered Moses had to pronounce judgment on the idolatrous worshipers and separate the profane from the acceptable. How many movement ministers today are willing to stand for what's right, even in the face of extreme pressure and ridicule? We must unequivocally be able to state that we are indeed on the Lord's side!

Those who chose idolatry were precluded from joining the congregation in worship ever again. I have heard many instances of ministries being put on hiatus or eliminated as a ministry of a church. Even if some dancers choose to rebel, the real responsibility rests on the shoulders of leadership. The proper teaching, training, and prevention of perversion will serve as protection for the dancers. Neglecting to uphold the Lord's instructions will only result in the movement being brought to a screeching halt.

Chapter 4

JEPHTHAH'S DAUGHTER

Certain dancers in the Scriptures remain nameless. Jephthah's daughter is one of them. There are several things that we discover about her, but her identity is closely attached with that of her father. Let's try to understand her background so that we can more completely grasp her plight.

In Judges Chapter 11, we are able to learn a bit of Jephthah's history. Born to a prostitute mother, his father Gilead raised him among his legitimate children. When his brothers grew older, he was ejected from his father's house by his brothers who insisted that he not inherit anything because of his lineage.

Gilead was married. Imagine what his wife had to go through! She was dealing with the aftermath of Gilead's decision while raising sons of her own. Did she fight for Jephthah, or was she relieved to finally rid herself of the reminder that her husband desired another?

Jephthah was forced to flee his childhood residence and ended up joining forces with companions described as "vain men." As a war was waged by the children of Ammon against Israel, his brothers called him back to serve as their leader. Because Jephthah was known as a man of valor, his brothers decided to cast aside their opinions of him when they felt Jephthah could benefit them by keeping them alive.

The Ammonites were descendants of Lot and his daughter by incest. After Sodom and Gomorrah were destroyed, both of Lot's daughters became pregnant by their father when he was intoxicated. Ammon and Moab were brothers and cousins whose father was also their grandfather. What a mess!

The Ammonites were used by God to deal with the children of Israel, who kept serving idol gods. The sons of Ammon served the false god Chemosh, whose name means "destroyer." Although God did not take pleasure in using the Ammonites to fight against His people, it must be noted that we can bring attacks on ourselves when we disobey the instructions of God. Even though Jephthah's presence had previously been a source of pain, his desire to be accepted prompted him to seize the opportunity to rule what once rejected him.

Jephthah decided to use the occasion to his advantage by being permanently received by his father's people as their leader. Seizing the moment, Jephthah entered into negotiations with the king of the children of Ammon, to no avail. In order to secure his victory against the Ammonites, Jephthah made the following vow to the Lord:

> **"If thou shalt without fail deliver the children of Ammon into mine hands, then it shall be, that whatsoever cometh forth of the doors of my house to meet me, when I return in peace from the children of Ammon, shall surely be the Lord's, and I will offer it up for a burnt offering."**
>
> – Judges 11:30-31

Did the Lord require Jephthah to make an additional promise? No. The Spirit of the Lord had already led him safely through the territory. Sometimes, our knowledge that the Lord is with us will cause us to try to take extra steps to determine a predictable outcome. Though Jephthah adhered to the tradition of offering up a sacrifice to God, the Lord's plan was already in operation. 2 Corinthians 3:6b lets us know *"For the letter killeth, but the spirit giveth life."* Jephthah was employing the law of sacrificial offerings in the presence of God, but were his motives pure?

Jephthah could have recognized that the Lord was already with him and obtained the victory. When we mix our personal desires in with what the Lord has empowered us to do, the end result can be disastrous. Jephthah won the battle, but lost something much greater.

Worship artists can also be faced with doing the same thing if the desire to uphold traditions takes precedence over submission to the Holy Spirit. Even though Jephthah's promise seemed righteous externally, his desire to be validated and vindicated caused him to get an insurance plan in case the move of God was not enough.

Jephthah was the victor. He returned home to celebrate, but soon discovered the gravity of his words:

> **"And Jephthah came to Mizpeh unto his house, and, behold, his daughter came out to meet him with timbrels and with dances: and she was his only child; beside her he had neither son nor daughter. And it came to pass, when he saw her, that he rent his clothes, and said, Alas, my daughter! thou hast brought me very low, and thou art one of them that trouble me: for I have opened my mouth unto the LORD, and I cannot go back."**
> — Judges 11:34-35

Because he made a vow, he had to honor it. As contrasted with Abraham and Isaac, there was no "ram in the bush" to deliver Jephthah from fulfilling his obligation. Unlike Abraham, the Lord did not request a sacrifice to be made by Jephthah.

This type of behavior was demonstrated by those who worshiped Chemosh, god of the Ammonites and Moabites. Moab was Ammon's brother/cousin. In 2 Kings 3:27, the King of Moab offered his oldest son as a burnt offering on the wall in an attempt to win a war against the Israelites. Human sac-rifice is often linked with the worship of false gods. Jephthah may not have intended to offer his daughter like a pagan, but his attempted manipulation of the outcome affected his bloodline.

When we desire to redeem ourselves instead of trusting the Lord completely, we can affect our future and legacy. Jephthah's decision had a direct impact on the life of his only child, a virgin daughter. Our deci-sions have consequences or rewards as well.

Jephthah's daughter was also one to embrace the traditions of her people. As was the custom of female relatives, she came out to meet her father with timbrels and dances. Take note that she is not described as carrying just one timbrel, but timbrels! Either this reveals to us that she was skilled at using more than one while dancing or that her companions were with her but are not mentioned. Her joyful ex-pression soon changed as her father blamed her for the deal that he had made.

It would have seemed normal that Jephthah was counting on seeing one of his animals upon his arrival. This would have been an easier sacrifice and may have appeared to be noble. Maybe he forgot that one of the traditions of the Israelite women included greeting victors by way of the dance. Had he become blinded by ambition to the point of forgetting the bigger picture? Maybe not.

He said, *"...whatsoever cometh forth of the doors of my house to meet me,"* in making a vow. The word house has more than one meaning in the Hebrew. It means an actual residence and also a shelter for animals. In essence, he was saying that anything was up for grabs! We must be careful with the promises we make.

Although she was affected by the vow her father made, she still submitted to his authority over her life. For two months, she was allowed to prepare for her death with the support of her friends. She then returned to her father to accept the consequences of his actions:

And it came to pass at the end of two months, that she returned unto her father, who did with her according to his vow which he had vowed: and she knew no man. And it was a custom in

Israel, that the daughters of Israel went yearly to lament the daughter of Jephthah the Gileadite four days in a year."

– Judges 11:39-40

Through the life of Mary, we learn of the virgin birth. For Jephthah's daughter, we learn of the virgin death. What a sad ending to what should have been celebrated as a new beginning!

Many who enter dance ministry do so innocently. Their motives may be pure as they are compelled to dance for the Father. Although this story may be viewed in a negative light, when we dance for our Heavenly Father, flesh must die! Because God is a Spirit, we must commune with Him spirit to Spirit.

We are expected to respond with joy when our Father makes His presence known. Jephthah's daughter did not wait for him to come to the place where she was—she came out to meet him! Some dancers may be required to leave the places they are and come to where God is! We must be willing to move from a familiar position into a place that causes us to be close to our Lord.

Because her father made a vow to the Lord, he could not break it, although it was devastating for him to carry out. Many of us make promises to God that may serve our own purposes. Praise God for His mercy covering every idle word that we may have spoken for which we did not suffer judgment. Be careful when making negotiations that the Lord does not ask for.

We are not aware of the girl's personal name, but we know that she defied her grandmother's legacy of prostitution by remaining a virgin. There is no specific mention of Jephthah's wife or how this child was conceived. What we are aware of is that he was responsible for raising her and also guilty of her demise. We are also held accountable for what we reproduce and what we destroy.

The decisions that parents make may impact generations. This can also apply to spiritual parents. For leaders, ambition and justification by any means necessary cannot work in conjunction with the Holy Spirit. It does not matter if we have been mistreated and feel as though we want to prove our worth to those who once rejected us. When we allow the Lord to handle it, we keep our own hands clean and our legacies alive!

Failing to ask the Lord what He wants can cancel a promising future. Let's not make sacrifices that are not required. What we give to the Lord comes with a promise of great returns. The price that we pay for self-ambition will only result in losses. We must choose our words and desires according to God's wisdom and direction.

Chapter 5

THE DAUGHTERS OF SHILOH

Even with valiant warriors, conquerors, and kings, the role of women has been very important throughout biblical times. The Benjamites realized how vital women were to society after they had been devastated by war. Every man, woman, and child had been slaughtered except for 600 young men of the tribe of Benjamin. They had no idea how their line would continue, seeing that there were no wives left.

The history became complex because of a promise made by the men of Israel. The Benjamites refused to give the men of Israel the person responsible for abusing the Levite's concubine. As a result, the Israelite men swore never to give a wife to the Benjamites from their daughters as evidenced in Judges 21:6-7:

"And the children of Israel grieved for Benjamin their brother, and said, 'One tribe is cut off from Israel today. What shall we do for wives for those who remain, seeing we have sworn by the LORD that we will not give them our daughters as wives?'"

The children of Israel could not overturn the oath that was made, so they had to figure out another way to find wives suitable for the Benjamites. They realized that no one from the Jabesh Gilead camp had come to the assembly when they made the oath, so they decided to rid all of the inhabitants from Jabesh Gilead who were not female virgins. Alerted, the remaining congregation proclaimed peace to the Benjamites and gave them additional women from Jabesh Gilead, but there were still not enough.

After counting them, they discovered that they had gained four hundred women, leaving them two hundred wives short. The elders of the congregation tried to figure out how the void would be filled for the two hundred men that were missing wives. They then remembered that there was a feast of the Lord held every year in Shiloh:

"Then they said, Behold, there is a feast of the LORD in Shiloh yearly in a place which is on the north side of Bethel, on the east side of the highway that goeth up from Bethel to Shechem, and on the south of Lebonah."

– Judges 21:19

They received clear directions concerning where to go. This particular feast is believed to have been the Feast of Tabernacles.[5] The people would return faithfully to Shiloh for this celebration. The children of Benjamin received further strategy in Judges 21:20-23:

Read

"Therefore they commanded the children of Benjamin, saying, Go and lie in wait in the vineyards; and see, and, behold, if the daughters of Shiloh come out to dance in dances, then come ye out of the vineyards, and catch you every man his wife of the daughters of Shiloh, and go to the land of Benjamin. And it shall be, when their fathers or their brethren come unto us to complain, that we will say unto them, be favourable unto them for our sakes: because we reserved not to each man his wife in the

---

[5] https://www.studylight.org/commentaries/bcc/judges-21.html

war: for ye did not give unto them at this time, that ye should be guilty. And the children of Benjamin did so, and took them wives, according to their number, of them that danced, whom they caught: and they went and returned unto their inheritance, and repaired the cities, and dwelt in them."

But wait! Weren't the daughters of Shiloh still a part of the children of Israel?

They found a loophole in the promise that they had made. Since they did not give the daughters of Shiloh to the Benjamites but the women were captured instead, this allowed them to gather the remaining two hundred and take them to their land as wives.

These women were not focused on getting male attention. Here again we see the societal tradition of dance being a regular part of the activities of women at celebrations in a community setting. They danced in dances, meaning that there were several steps involved and a cooperative disposition needed to dance together as a unit.

It is interesting to note that the daughters of Shiloh that danced had to be virgins to meet the qualifications of the children of Benjamin. This denotes a need for purity in the dance and obedience to a lifestyle of righteousness. It was literally their season or time to dance. Other biblical accounts of women dancing as a community included all of the women of Israel or women coming out of cities. The daughters of Shiloh were distinct in that they were unmarried and shared a common bond as a group.

So, why was Shiloh significant? Shiloh means *peaceful* or *tranquil, a place of rest.* It was an assembly place for the Israelites where the Ark of the Covenant was stationed until it was captured by the Philistines.

> **"And the whole congregation of the children of Israel assembled together at Shiloh, and set up the tabernacle of the congregation there. And the land was subdued before them."**
>
> – Joshua 18:1

We see that the presence of the Lord was what gathered the people to worship at Shiloh yearly. Later, we are informed of the sin that caused an opportunity for the enemy to come in and disconnect them from God's presence:

> "Now Israel went out to battle against the Philistines, and encamped beside Ebenezer; and the Philistines encamped in Aphek. Then the Philistines put themselves in battle array against Israel. And when they joined battle, Israel was defeated by the Philistines, who killed about four thousand men of the army in the field. And when the people had come into the camp, the elders of Israel said, 'Why has the LORD defeated us today before the Philistines? Let us bring the ark of the covenant of the LORD from Shiloh to us, that when it comes among us it may save us from the hand of our enemies.' So the people sent to Shiloh, that they might bring from there the ark of the covenant of the LORD of hosts, who dwells between the cherubim. And the two sons of Eli, Hophni and Phinehas, were there with the ark of the covenant of God."
>
> – 1 Samuel 4:1-4

Hophni and Phineas were the sons of Eli, the priest. This was the same Eli that trained the prophet Samuel, but his own sons were corrupt and brought judgment on themselves as priests without correction.

Leaders can find themselves vulnerable when they show favoritism or refuse to give correction to someone based on relationship. Those who have been entrusted with care for the people cannot allow those placed in positions of leadership to abuse the trust that has been granted. Even when church and dance leaders allow rampant sin to continue, they invite the rapid departure of the presence of the Lord from among them.

Israel assumed that because the presence of the Lord brought them victory through the use of the Ark before, that they could assume it would work again, even without seeking Him first:

"So the Philistines fought, and Israel was defeated, and every man fled to his tent. There was a very great slaughter, and there fell of Israel thirty thousand foot soldiers. Also the ark of God was captured; and the two sons of Eli, Hophni and Phinehas, died."

— 1 Samuel 4:10-11

We cannot use the Lord merely when it is convenient for us.

Just because a dance worked before does not mean that it will have the same impact in a different situation. We must seek the Lord each and every time that we go into enemy territory, even if we think that we are strong enough to face opposition. Previous victories do not guarantee future successes.

After hearing of the death of his sons, Eli fell down backward and broke his neck and died due to his age and weight. The fall of a leader can have grave consequences. Eli served as a judge for 40 years but neglected to correct his own sons.

The story did not end there. This epic defeat brought even further repercussions:

"Now his daughter-in-law, Phinehas' wife, was with child, due to be delivered; and when she heard the news that the ark of God was captured, and that her father-in-law and her husband were dead, she bowed herself and gave birth, for her labor pains came upon her. And about the time of her death the women who stood by her said to her, 'Do not fear, for you have borne a son.' But she did not answer, nor did she regard it. Then she named

the child Ichabod, saying, 'The glory has departed from Israel!' because the ark of God had been captured and because of her father-in-law and her husband. And she said, 'The glory has departed from Israel, for the ark of God has been captured.'"

— 1 Samuel 4:19-22

The next generation did not experience the presence of God because of what the leaders allowed. This still happens in many churches today. The presence of the Lord has long departed but the people still gather there.

The Ark never returned to Shiloh. Did the women continue to dance where the presence of the Lord was not? There are many dancing today that do so out of tradition and obligation, but the Lord is not with them. Though disobedience caused the presence of the Lord to leave the place where it had been for hundreds of years, it would not be the last time we saw God's presence being used in the context of dance as David would demonstrate.

Wickedness will cause us to lose His presence! The Lord made Himself very clear regarding Shiloh in Jeremiah 7:12-14:

"'But go now to My place which was in Shiloh, where I set My name at the first, and see what I did to it because of the wickedness of My people Israel. And now, because you have done all these works,' says the LORD, 'and I spoke to you, rising up early and speaking, but you did not hear, and I called you, but you did not answer, therefore I will do to the house which is called by My name, in which you trust, and to this place which I gave to you and your fathers, as I have done to Shiloh.'"

Sin resulted in the absence of glory! Ministries that operate today without regard to lifestyle and behavior may find themselves engaging in traditions without triumph. They showed more faithfulness to the location of worship than to the God who deserves it.

It is not impossible for the people of God to become wicked. The Lord lets us know that He can speak to people who choose to ignore Him. Becoming immune to God's instructions evicts His glory.

Presently in Shiloh, there is a synagogue that has been built as a replica of the biblical tabernacle.[6] Many dance ministries of today also make replicas of dances, garments, and traditions without seeking the Lord first. We cannot settle for having a form of godliness and resist God Himself.

Like the daughters of Shiloh, we can dance for years out of tradition and celebrate according to the law. We must be honest and ask ourselves if we are willing to confront sin in order to keep the presence of God with us. If not, we will dance to songs and meet at locations that God has promised never to return.

---

[6] https://www.visions-israel.com/modernmishkan

Chapter 6

WOMEN

The first mention of dance in the Scriptures often highlights Miriam celebrating with jubilation, timbrel in hand and a song in her mouth. What is often missed or overlooked is that all of the women joined her by the masses. In fact, all of the women followed her lead.

These women were not distinguished by age, marital status, or skill level. As a community, the women submitted themselves to a leader and submitted to each other for them to be able to dance as a unit.

"And Miriam the prophetess, the sister of Aaron, took a timbrel in her hand; and all the women went out after her with timbrels and with dances. And Miriam answered them, Sing ye to the LORD, for he hath triumphed gloriously; the horse and his rider hath he thrown into the sea."

– Exodus 15:20-21

Not only did they dance collectively, they played timbrels as instruments and sang with their voices. If they already came prepared with timbrels, this suggests that dancing was a regularly practiced part of the Hebrew culture. They also sang as a united chorus.

Many dancers today are encouraged to only focus on the movement and eliminate mouthing or singing any words. While the standard tradition of structured dance training discourages dancers from singing, we must be careful when we impose strict requirements on Christian dancers that the Bible shows as an acceptable practice. In order to follow the established biblical model, we must caution against making our personal preferences apply to an entire movement discipline.

As there were no electrical or portable sound systems or musical recordings then, dancers had to provide the music and lyrics along with the movement. In essence, this allowed them to speak the Word as opposed to merely listening to it. They came into agreement with the prophetic word being released by leadership at God's direction.

This tradition is also apparent in other biblical accounts. David was greeted by multitudes of singing and dancing female musicians in 1 Samuel 18:6-7:

"And it came to pass as they came, when David was returned from the slaughter of the Philistine, that the women came out of all cities of Israel, singing and dancing, to meet king Saul, with tabrets, with joy, and with instruments of musick. And the women answered one another as they played, and said, Saul hath slain his thousands, and David his ten thousands."

Talk about unity in the community! Imagine the number of women streaming in from the surrounding territories, celebrating with joyful abandon and dancing with fervor! Since they had a common focus, they were able to operate as a unit.

In order to know that it was time to respond rhythmically to a victory, the women must have heard about David's triumphant win in advance. There was no social media, telephones, or mail delivery service then. This means that they had a system of communication that allowed the news to reach the entire region. As it is often said, the best form of advertisement is word of mouth!

Here again we have the women playing instruments while singing and dancing. In this case, the description moves beyond the tabret and includes other musical instruments. The tabret and timbrel are described as wooden instruments covered with animal skin, set with bells of brass. The Hebrew word for the timbrel and tabret is **toph**.

The other musical instruments are not described in detail, but in order for the women to dance with them, they would have had to have been portable. We also discover that musicians were not limited to men, but women played as well. It is also good to note that they were saying the same thing, or agreeing about the purpose of the celebration. Whenever lyrical dance is being presented, it is imperative that dancers know the words to the songs to move with an understanding.

It would seem as though everyone would have been happy about this flash mob that assembled in David's honor, but that was not the case. These women were bragging about another man at the king's party! The word "played" here also means laughing and mocking, in addition to the actual playing of a musical instrument.

The Bible says that they came to meet King Saul, but David received greater accolades for defeating tens of thousands while they discussed Saul being victorious over thousands. King Saul may have sensed that he was being mocked by women from whom he desired admiration. Saul was furious!

"And Saul was very wroth, and the saying displeased him; and he said, They have ascribed unto David ten thousands, and to me they have ascribed but thousands: and what can he have more but the kingdom? And Saul eyed David from that day and forward."

– 1 Samuel 18:8-9

It is a sad day when leaders lose the respect of those who follow them. Whispers of a change in dance ministry leadership due to failure or transition can cause suspicion, jealousy, envy, and rivalries. The way that the women behaved in front of an audience caused a private reaction that eventually became public.

Women dancing for men is not a new concept. Notice here that this was also not necessarily an instance of Godly worship. They were praising the accomplishments of David and Saul, but nothing was said about the Lord. The king could not stand to be made fun of in his own domain. As a result, Saul became instantly envious of David because of this demonstration and an evil spirit tormented him. Saul was on a mission to take David's life!

This scene became widely known and was even used to identify David later in 1 Samuel 21:10-11:

"And David arose and fled that day for fear of Saul, and went to Achish the king of Gath. And the servants of Achish said unto him, is not this David the king of the land? did they not sing one to another of him in dances, saying, Saul hath slain his thousands, and David his ten thousands?"

The voices of these women carried a lot of influence! David had to run for cover to another leader who would protect him and not kill him.

Too often, I have had to counsel dance ministry leaders who were suffering persecution at the hands of leadership. Even though there are several instances of dancers gone "rogue," there are also legitimate instances of leaders who are threatened by the impact that effective movement ministry has on a congregation.

Many dancers have had to search for a new church to be able to continue dancing. Others have felt that the pressure was too strong, and have decided to take a sabbatical. David experienced conflict due to the dance on more than one occasion. This is not a coincidence.

Dance is a powerful tool that can generate substantial backlash. These women came into agreement and David's fame spread throughout the land. David was probably not prepared for the response of Saul to their admiration.

Someone will always have an opinion of us, whether positive or negative. If we don't expect conversations to foster hazardous working conditions, we can be blindsided.

Envy, ridicule, and misunderstandings are to be expected. Know that the Word will provide protection and direction when in need of rescue.

Although David was not personally responsible for the women dancing and infuriating the king, it was a life-changing dance nevertheless. Many worshipers seek to impact lives through song and movement. If we are not careful, we can invite evil to arise when our focus is on man and not God. Although many describe this scene as a prophetic dance, it also shows the danger of making a mockery of Kingdom principles in public. No ruling king wants to be dishonored.

This dance was considered prophetic because David returned from the slaughter of the Philistine. David, not yet king, was considered greater than Saul, the reigning ruler. If we allow ourselves to listen to the words of people, we too can be tempted with envy due to comparison.

We must cast down every thought that would allow us to covet the prophetic word given to another ministry, leader, or region. As artists, we have each received our own measure. While we can multiply what we have been given, there will always be someone who exceeds us. Instead of making them an enemy, we can become a student or servant.

Saul was still king, and yet the servants of Achish were giving David publicity! Again, this dance became nationwide news as the word continued to be spread in 1 Samuel 29:5:

"Is not this David, of whom they sang one to another in dances, saying, Saul slew his thousands, and David his ten thousands?"

The princes of the Philistines were discussing David's fame by recalling the dancing women and decided that he would be unable to go with them into battle. David was forced to leave even though he had served faithfully because his reputation could not overshadow the princes of the Philistines. They probably did not want the women to come out again and dance about David instead of themselves.

People can and will be insecure. Our goal must be not to diminish the work of God through us because of the opinions of others. We too may have areas that need transformation in our minds. Some people would like to relate to David, but their actions are more like those of Saul. These women were a key element in the preparation that David would face as a leader. Who is talking about you?

Chapter 7

MEN

Although one of the few references to men dancing is highlighted by the radical leaping and twirling done by David, he was not alone. Dancing has always been an acceptable expression during times of celebration and as a response to a victory in battle. Entire groups of people are mentioned dancing and men are no exception.

Let's examine one such occasion in the Book of 1 Samuel. The Amalekites invaded Ziklag and had taken the women captive. David and his men arrived and discovered that all of their wives and children had been taken. Did David make a valiant declaration and run off to be a hero? No. David and the men cried so hard until they could shed no more tears.

Although sometimes our first response may be to run into battle, there are times when our emotions will overwhelm us. Even with all of David's notable victories, he experienced some setbacks as a leader that not only affected him but all of the people who followed him. It got so intense for David that his own people wanted to stone him because they had suffered this terrible loss. Instead of allowing the complaints of men to destroy him, David encouraged himself in the Lord.

His next step was to go directly to God and inquire of Him. David understood that although he was skilled in war and had been recently celebrated by thousands of women for his accomplishments through dancing and singing, without the Lord's permission, he was doomed to fail.

> **"And David enquired at the Lord, saying, Shall I pursue after this troop? shall I overtake them? And he answered him, Pursue: for thou shalt surely overtake them, and without fail recover all."**
> – 1 Samuel 30:8

David refused to take one single step without God's permission! How many dancers and movement artists consult the Lord before making a move?

David and his men set out to perform a repossession of all that belonged to them. With 400 men, David advanced. On the way, David encountered an Egyptian that had been left in the field, weak because of sickness. After feeding him, David discovered that he was the servant of an Amalekite. David struck an agreement that he would not kill the servant or deliver him to his master if he would lead him to where the Amalikites camped.

David arrived on the scene and discovered dancing troops in action:

"And when he had brought him down, behold, they were spread abroad upon all the earth, eating and drinking, and dancing, because of all the great spoil that they had taken out of the land of the Philistines, and out of the land of Judah."

– 1 Samuel 30:16

The word used for dancing here is **chagag**, (Strong's #2287) meaning *feast, dance,* and *stagger*. It also means *to reel or be giddy*, used in the context of being drunk. This type of dance describes the kind done at festivals, which included an atmosphere of eating and drinking. As a tradition, most parties today include food, drinks, and dancing. David took full advantage of this distraction and conquered them from twilight until the next day.

It is important for us to note that the Amalekites were descendants of Esau, Jacob's twin brother, and at other times, his enemy. Even though the Lord's instructions in the Bible were to destroy the Amalekites, a remnant was spared that caused continual controversy with Israel. This can apply to areas in our lives that will continue to work against us if they are not eradicated.

In the arts, the fight is often with the flesh. Infighting can usually be found within the ranks of worshipers that were birthed into similar assignments. Competition then creates confusion. Instead of focusing on complete dedication to the service of the Lord, personal preservation often provokes division that is long-lasting.

The Amalekite men were wiped out at a dance. They were not worshiping the Lord but celebrating themselves by capturing the wives and children of other men. In modern culture, women are frequently portrayed as dancing to please men, while men are often depicted as using dance to "battle" other men.

For many decades, "street" dancers have been known to battle each other through break dancing, crumping, hip-hop and other masculine movements. Although women have been incorporated in later times, these types of standoffs were comprised mostly of males. Whether on urban streets or on the club dance floor, these turf wars were settled by the applause of the crowd.

This tradition can be viewed in many dance movies that show teams of men warring with movement. Although the original concept is tribal in nature and precedes modern times, cinema continues to capitalize on the need to see war in whatever form it appears. Television has also been a major platform for dance team competitions and personal dance battle wins. These videos can be found on social media as well.

Although many worship artists would like to promote that they only dance, sing, and shout for the glory of the Lord, there are people who dance for sporting events, birthday celebrations, special parties, and celebratory occasions. Motives matter.

If we are not yielded to God concerning our possessions and battles, we will find ourselves in a vulnerable position, ripe for a takeover. The men danced, but who was watching the camp? The enemy knows how to dance as well. As people of God, we must understand that there is a time to dance, but there is also a time to fight!

Although this victory was promised by God, we can learn a vital lesson here. Many dance and worship arts ministries concern themselves with activity and forget to put safeguards in place. We cannot take on the nature of the enemy by celebrating ourselves and fighting the people of God. David used wisdom to defeat the enemy and had the Lord on his side. Dance was created by God, but can be also used to glorify self.

Scripture says that the men were spread abroad over the land. Even though they may have been numerous, this also indicates that there was disorganization and a lack of order. Having this type of atmosphere opens up our ministries to experience defeat. If we conduct ourselves like a bunch of unstable, drunken individuals, it will be hard to defend ourselves against attacks. These tactics are not just physical in nature. A bad reputation can kill the effectiveness of a ministry.

It was characteristic of soldiers and fighters to dance. Although David's dance was described in a different context, men danced nevertheless. It is no wonder why sports, boxing, and racing events cause many men to leap up and down in response. The thrill of victory is often followed by matching gestures. Men who dance for themselves may experience defeat, but those who move according to God's instructions will be guaranteed victory.

Chapter 8

DAVID

If David entered a "Most Popular Biblical Dancer" contest, he would be most likely to win. Preachers, writers, and artists have celebrated the accomplishments of David time and again. We have often heard that this aggressive man of God "danced out of his clothes" from pulpits and people worldwide. Are we absolutely sure that we are telling his triumphant story accurately? 2 Samuel 6:14 zooms in on a radical scene:

"And David danced before the Lord with all his might; and David was girded with a linen ephod."

King David was leaping and dancing before the Lord with power and strength! Many of us quote this passage, but what initially happened that prompted this verse to begin with the word **"And…?"**

2 Samuel Chapter 6 tells us about the time when David desired to bring the Ark

of the Covenant to the City of David. The ark had been captured and was away from the people of God, so David wanted to bring it back to the place of restoration. He gathered a group of people and made preparations to have a great procession.

David ordered a new cart, assembled a large band that played several different types of instruments, and conducted the parade! With the help of oxen, they marched forward, playing and celebrating along the parade route. Suddenly, there was an interruption and traffic came to a complete stop. The oxen stumbled. David's friend Uzzah noticed that the ark was about to fall! He quickly reached out his hand to steady it. Uzzah was not moving. What happened?

Uzzah made a fatal error and the anger of God struck him. David was upset and decided to cancel the festivities immediately. David questioned how the ark could come to him when he had already tried and failed. He decided to store it at Obededom's house until he could figure out which steps to take next.

Three months passed. David heard how Obededom and his entire household were blessed. David then went to retrieve the ark and begin the procession yet again. But this time, things were different.

1 Chronicles 15 gives a different version of the same event. King David reminded the people that the Levites were the chosen ones for transporting the Ark of God. They were to carry it on staves or poles and not on a cart. Although the Levites were designated to carry it, David gathered the entire nation of Israel to Jerusalem to celebrate the arrival of the ark along with him.

David confessed that there was a mistake made the first time because they did not handle the ark according to the order that the Lord commanded. The Levites and the priests set themselves apart and carried the ark on their shoulders into the city. Singing, instrumentation, and great rejoicing ensued. David himself led the processional in dance. Some even claim that David danced out of his clothes, but did he really?

Before we reach a decision, let's compare each of the two accounts and arrive at a biblical conclusion:

"And David danced before the Lord with all his might; and David was girded with a linen ephod."

– 2 Samuel 6:14

Gird means *to fasten* or *secure with a belt, to surround*.[7] Linen was a type of fabric created from the flax plant. The priests wore garments made of fine linen for the purposes of service and worship.

The ephod was a priestly garment or outer covering. Ordinary priests wore white linen ephods, while the high priest wore an ephod with more costly adornments of gold, blue, scarlet, and purple. These uniquely exquisite garments also included a designer shoulder piece and an additional breastplate containing gold and jewels.

David wore the simple white linen garment, which was considered to be inferior to that of the high priest.

"Then David returned to bless his household. And Michal the daughter of Saul came out to meet David, and said, How glorious was the king of

---

[7]
https://www.blueletterbible.org/lang/Lexicon/Lexicon.cfm?strongs=H2296&t=KJV

Israel to day, who uncovered himself to day in the eyes of the handmaids of his servants, as one of the vain fellows shamelessly uncovereth himself! And David said unto Michal, It was before the LORD, which chose me before thy father, and before all his house, to appoint me ruler over the people of the LORD, over Israel: therefore will I play before the LORD. And I will yet be more vile than thus, and will be base in mine own sight: and of the maid-servants which thou hast spoken of, of them shall I be had in honour."

— 2 Samuel 6:20-22

If David was wearing a linen ephod, why did his wife use the word "uncovered?" This word in the Hebrew means *to reveal, uncover, remove,* or *be discovered.*[8] Another definition means *to uncover nakedness.* Was King David leaping and dancing so vigorously that his clothes fell off? Let's compare this passage of text with the next description found in 1 Chronicles 15:27-29:

---

[8]

https://www.blueletterbible.org/lang/Lexicon/Lexicon.cfm?strongs=H1540&t=KJV

"And David was clothed with a robe of fine linen, and all the Levites that bare the ark, and the singers, and Chenaniah the master of the song with the singers: David also had upon him an ephod of linen. Thus all Israel brought up the ark of the covenant of the Lord with shouting, and with sound of the cornet, and with trumpets, and with cymbals, making a noise with psalteries and harps. And it came to pass, as the ark of the covenant of the Lord came to the city of David, that Michal, the daughter of Saul looking out at a window saw king David dancing and playing: and she despised him in her heart."

Wait… Aren't there more clothes listed here? David was clothed with a robe of fine linen and wore a linen ephod. Clothed in the Hebrew (**karbel** Strong's #3736) means *to put a mantle on,* not to take one off. The robe was a garment worn over a tunic by men of rank. This sleeveless garment was long, wide, and extended down to the ankles.

In addition to the standard linen, David had on a robe of fine linen, which was created from byssus, a fine cloth that was used in the ephod of the high priest.[9] Traditionally, linen came from the flax plant while byssus was derived from a sea mollusk. Byssus was also known as "sea silk." The Earth includes the land and the seas. David was symbolically used to bring unity to what had been separated!

Byssus was also used in the garments of kings. The standard linen garment worn by priests was on David along with the fine linen garment traditionally worn by the king. The kingship and priesthood were coming together! What a divine precursor to the entrance of Jesus as both King and High Priest!

During the procession, the entire company of Levites, singers, musicians, and the choir director were all dressed alike. This is how many traditional choirs and ensembles embraced the choir robe and the uniform. It was a sign of unity and kept the focus on worship unto God.

Noticed that the text says that Michal despised David. She regarded him with contempt in her heart. Another definition of despise means *to trample with the feet*. While

---

[9] https://biblehub.com/nlt/exodus/28-6.htm

David used his feet to dance before the Lord, Michal attempted to crush David with her words in a manipulative attempt to stop his feet from moving.

In 2 Samuel Chapter 6, Michal compared David to one of the "vain fellows" that uncovered himself. I am pretty confident that public nakedness was not a common sight on the City of David streets. Vain means *worthless or poor*. Shamelessly has the same meaning in Hebrew as uncovered! This indicates an attitude more than an action.

We see this confirmed through David's response, *"And I will yet be more vile than thus, and will be base in mine own sight..."* **Vile** means *to be swift* and *to be of little account or reputation*. **Base** means *to be humble, low, or humiliated*. The one thing David definitely took off that day was his kingly title, making himself equal to the common man in the sight of God.

1 Chronicles 15 includes no mention of David being naked or uncovered. Is this a contradiction? I don't think so. If David did "dance out of his clothes," it is not found in the Scriptures between these two accounts. Michal regarded his actions as foolish and

having no value. If we do not call David a fool for dancing, why should we refer to him as naked?

As the King's wife, Michal may have felt that David's position was too important to be out in the streets, dressed as a commoner. Traditionally, kings wore elaborate robes. There was no such garment here. Instead of David drawing attention to himself as king, he focused his display on the Lord as the true King of the people.

Michal's outburst would cost her dearly. We are informed that she did not have a child for the rest of her life. After this account, we would see her name no more.

Instead of joyfully greeting him with a dance as was customary for the returning victor, she became negative towards him in the same way that her father Saul had. Saul eyed David after the women danced. Saul's daughter despised King David right after he danced. Some things definitely run in the family!

David describes what the Lord has done for him in regards to dance in Psalm 30:11-12:

"Thou hast turned for me my mourning into dancing: thou hast put off my sackcloth, and girded me with gladness; To the end that my glory may sing praise to thee, and not be silent. O LORD my God, I will give thanks unto thee forever."

Dancing is the opposite of mourning. His tears turned into rejoicing and his garments metaphorically changed from funeral garb to celebration attire.

In the presence of the Lord is fullness of joy! David expressed his dance in such a way that all honor would go to God and none to himself. This should always be the position of the worshiper before the Lord.

David also embraced the total package as a worshiper with the marriage of both music and dance. As a musician, David's skillful playing relieved King Saul from the torment that he had experienced. David's anointing for penning powerful lyrics and music is noted throughout the Psalms.

As David wrote the words that detailed his triumphs and tragedies, he instructed the Chief Musician about which instruments to play, and in what style it should be done. David also appointed musicians and singers to serve the Lord. It was a corporate operation.

From these recurring examples, we now understand that dance is just as valid an expression of worship and praise as music and singing. In many congregations today, dance is still being challenged in terms of its acceptability. This rebuttal should be expected as we see music and singing emphasized more often in the Scriptures, while dance has caused envy, ridicule, conflict, and even the death of a prophet.

If music can be powerful enough to bring about deliverance in a person's life, the dances that are set to it can be just as effective. David did not exclude dance from his offering before the Lord. The church must resist the spirit of Michal and truly embrace the spirit of David.

Chapter 9

CHILDREN

Although there is a myriad of lists in terms of births in the Bible, we do not really get a good glimpse of what role children played concerning dance in the Bible. Several accounts of men and women dancing are available, as well as gatherings of cultural groups of people. What about the children?

Job 21:11-12 mentions a group of children dancing, but not in the most positive light:

"They send forth their little ones like a flock, and their children dance. They take the timbrel and harp, and rejoice at the sound of the organ."

Sounds like a scene right out of a church service, right? Actually, Job is describing the wicked. The meaning of children here is used to describe a group of young boys or males being sent out to dance. Gesenuis' Hebrew-Chaldee Lexicon defines this group

of little ones as *evil and ungodly*. The definition of the word children in this context is
less gender-specific. Though it refers to a
son, it also means offspring, descendants,
and youth.

The Hebrew word for dance used in Job
21 is **raqad**, meaning *to skip about, to leap,*
and *to make to skip*. There is something
slightly contagious about dancing that in-
spires others to get up and join in! Though
some would want to believe that biblical
dance was always done in a worship context,
this is not truc. Unbelievers also embraced
dance as a communal form of expression
and as a response to celebration.

Though many would like to restrict the
timbrel to an instrument used by women,
we see its presence outside of the traditional
female dance circles. Many tambourines
used today are still identified as instruments
of praise, but this scene reveals that those
outside of the faith danced, played instruments, and celebrated with them. If the
actions are the same, how can we distin-
guish between a praise and a party? Both the
intention and the instruction will separate
the holy from the profane.

There is a raging debate growing concerning the use of items in worship that are perceived to be ungodly in origin. Some of the common items up for discussion are paraphernalia used by belly dancers, painted faces in mime, dance fans, and more. While I am not going to debate the argument on behalf of either side, the Encyclopaedia Britannica reveals that the timbrel was used in Egypt, Mesopotamia, Greece, Rome, and Israel. Several cultures used it. It was described as being used in rituals in ancient Sumer as well.

While we must be aware of the original intent for something, we must also keep this in mind:

> **"For by Him were all things created, that are in heaven, and that are in earth, visible and invisible, whether they be thrones, or dominions, or principalities, or powers: all things were created by him, and for him."**
> – Colossians 1:16

We must continue to come to Him like little children, remaining innocent and pure in our worship towards Him.

Even for very small children, a natural response to music is to dance. When a child loses his or her natural response to music, it may be evidence of a deeper problem. Jesus describes such an instance:

> **"But whereunto shall I liken this generation? It is like unto children sitting in the markets, and calling unto their fellows, and saying, We have piped unto you, and ye have not danced; we have mourned unto you, and ye have not lamented."**
> — Matthew 11:16-17

The word children here means *little boy* or *lad*. This supports the tradition of gender separation in Hebraic and Jewish dance.

The marketplace was a gathering location for all kinds of business transactions. Were these youth simply hanging around the premises? Were they apprentices? Did their families conduct business at this location? This group is being described as familiar enough to call out to their friends (or fellows) who were present along with them.

The playing of the flute should have ignited a response through movement, but there was none. The dance (defined here as

orcheomai in Hebrew) should have been an upbeat, rapid style. The piper's reward for his melody was movement, but there was no payday. To further highlight this lack of reaction, He states that they sang sad songs of mourning, but there was no emotional response. The normal, usual behavior patterns that should have accompanied these scenarios were strangely absent.

What causes a generation to resist the dance? Until fairly recent times, multiple churches and organizations have routinely shunned the ministry of dance or restricted it to special occasions. This is especially evident during the Holiday seasons.

Jesus' presence should have been openly welcomed with celebration, but there were those who refused to accept Him as the Messiah. Luke recalls hearing about the same instance:

> **"And the Lord said, Whereunto then shall I liken the men of this generation? And to what are they like? They are like unto children sitting in the marketplace, and calling one to another, and saying, We have piped unto you, and ye have not danced; we have**

mourned to you, and ye have not wept."

— Luke 7:31-32

Luke's word choices are slightly different, but very significant! Instead of referring to the generation as young lads, he described them as "men," which is a neutral term from the Greek word **anthropos**, meaning *human beings, male or female.* Its context speaks more to the sinful nature of them than to their physical attributes.

He also used a different word to describe the children! **Paidion** in the Greek includes both boys and girls. How can two people walk with the Lord, hear the same thing, and yet interpret it differently? Matthew was a tax collector and Luke was a physician. We could surmise that Matthew was accustomed to viewing people as units, while Luke saw them as individuals.

In a patriarchal system, the roles of women are less defined and often viewed as less significant. Medical professionals served the needs of both men and women and the differences must be understood in order to care for them properly.

Was this the old system versus an emerging one? Mary's role in the birth of Jesus was so significant that we hear no more of Joseph's name after the childhood of Jesus. In terms of dance and movement, what was once separated by distinction of the flesh was now becoming one by the Spirit.

Men became like children. What was once restricted had been opened. Jesus warned us not to be resistant to the change that He was bringing to the religious order of the day.

Many children's dance and movement ministries have been launched and continue to spread in the churches and communities. Unlike these children, they must be trained to recognize the appropriate time to dance and how to respond to truth when it is present. If we want this generation to have a greater impact in spreading the Good News through movement, they must be trained to recognize and embrace the knowledge of when the time is right for dancing.

Chapter 10

"THEM"

"Them." "They." "People." These are some
of the mysterious descriptions used to identify groups of unknowns. To delve a bit
further into this particular set of dancers, we
have to consider the source of the commen-
tary.

We find "them" in the Psalms. Psalm
149:1-3 makes an introduction by an un-
identified writer:

> **"Praise ye the LORD. Sing unto the
> LORD a new song, and His praise in
> the congregation of saints. Let Israel
> rejoice in Him that made him: let the
> children of Zion be joyful in their
> King. Let them praise His name in the
> dance: let them sing praises unto Him
> with the timbrel and harp."**

The word used for praise here is **halal** in
Hebrew, meaning *to shine* (of God's favor), *to
flash forth light, to boast.* Not only is this visual,

but audible as well. Praise can be seen and heard!

The writer gives several instructions for how this praise should be demonstrated, almost like verbal choreography. He lets us know that this praise is to be directed to the Lord.

Song selection is also important. The people are instructed to sing a new or fresh song, meaning one that has not been sung or heard before. It was common biblically to see dancers singing and playing instruments while moving simultaneously. Today, most dance ministries select songs that have been previously recorded and are available on the market for sale and distribution.

Spontaneous dance can take place during an impromptu worship or praise song. This is more common in churches that have already embraced congregational worship. A dancer that is comfortable with movement and understands how to flow in worship can appear to have rehearsed even though the song is unfamiliar.

The writer instructs the people to sing a tehillah praise song, which includes adoration and thanksgiving to the Lord. This was not to be done privately, but in front of the general congregation or assembly. This was not for performance, but participation.

He then identifies who should be rejoicing. He encourages Israel to be glad. Notice that the text says **"rejoice in him that made him!"** Israel's name (the actual man) was changed from Jacob, meaning *supplanter* (or one who seizes something illegally), to Israel, meaning, "God prevails." Although Jacob initially prevailed against his twin Esau in the womb, ultimately, the Lord would prevail in the end.

Why would the author refer to Israel the man instead of the children of Israel? The Lord is the Beginning and the End. The transformation of Israel signified the changing of an old nature into a new one. Yes, the children of Israel danced, but without this change there would be no true movement.

The children of Zion, or Jerusalem can now join in! This same Jerusalem was also the City of David and the place where Jesus entered as King. Prophetically, all of the offspring from Israel to David to Jesus were to be joyful in their King!

Gesenius' Lexicon defines joyful as the Hebrew word **giyl**, meaning, *to go in a circle, to leap for joy, to tremble,* and *to dance.* This was done in response to their King. Present-day dancers must be able to confess that the ultimate leader is Christ the King and we must take joy in Him.

The directive is then given to "let them praise His name in the dance." Not only are they to praise the King, but also call Him by name. If we are to fully acknowledge who we are submitting to in our praise and worship, we must be careful when excluding His name from songs or lyrics. In our growing accommodation of non-offensive sensitivity, we will be invited to omit songs that include the name of Jesus in public presentations. Will you bow to the pressure or say the name of your King?

The Hebrew word for dance in this Psalm is **machowl**, simply meaning *to dance.* Combining this with the joyful giyl, we are able to see an amazing choreography develop with several different movement styles incorporated. What a sight to behold!

We continue to go further as we witness the inclusion of singing and instruments into the scene along with the timbrel and harp. Once again, we see dance, singing, and instruments being utilized together. The Hebrew word for sing in Psalm 149 is **zamar**, meaning *to sing, play on a musical instrument, to dance*! Why have we made these expressions exclusive of one another in the congregational setting?

The timbrel or tambourine was to be beaten while the stringed harp was played. It is interesting to note that Miriam is often associated with the timbrel while David was skilled with the harp. Both of these dance leaders represented the prophetic—Miriam the prophetess and David the prophetic Psalmist; they were both musicians— Miriam's timbrel and David's harp; both were lyrical—Miriam sang while she danced and David wrote songs. The depiction of male and female here helps us to embrace that "them" includes both genders for the purposes of dance.

Psalm 150:4 selects different words but essentially paints a similar picture:

"Praise Him with the timbrel and dance: praise Him with stringed instruments and organs."

Amid the command to praise the Lord with several instruments present, the timbrel and dance are listed as suitable ways to praise.

Dance here is the original Hebrew word **machowl**, which is a general term for dancing. In addition to the stringed instruments, the organs were pipes or reeds requiring breath to function. Different than what we understand as a church organ today, these instruments were able to fit in the hand and were easily movable during times of open celebration.

What a noise they must have made! The trumpets, bagpipes, stringed instruments, tambourines, and cymbals were all listed… but wait! Dance was included in the list of instruments as well.

The beginning of Psalm 150 identifies where the Lord was to be praised.

"Praise ye the LORD. Praise God in His sanctuary: praise Him in the firmament of His power."
– Psalm 150:1

The next verses define the purpose for the praise:

"Praise him for his mighty acts: praise him according to his excellent greatness."

— Psalm 150:2

We then see the mighty orchestra:

"Praise him with the sound of the trumpet: praise him with the psaltery and harp. Praise him with the timbrel and dance: praise him with stringed instruments and organs. Praise him upon the loud cymbals: praise him upon the high sounding cymbals."

— Psalm 150:3-5

Dance itself is an instrument! It can make sounds (stomping, clapping), needs breath to operate, and requires hands and feet, just like many instruments. Dance belongs with the instruments. There is no argument.

Dancers in the Old Testament were responsible for providing their own personal music. They were also singers and musicians with knowledge of the skill needed to be proficient.

Finally, the contributors of the praise are revealed:

"Let everything that hath breath praise the LORD. Praise ye the LORD."
— Psalm 150:6

Breath in this context means both *breath* and *spirit* (including that of God and man). This Scripture not only tells us to let others praise Him, but for the listener and reader to join in as well.

Praise is not passive and worship is not worrisome. The Bible consistently shows unity in the dances of women, men, and nations via public demonstrations. Dance is not just reserved for the classically trained. It is a vital instrument to be used in the corporate expression of praise for all!

If we are to bless the Lord at all times, should we dance at all times? Ecclesiastes 3 gives us some parameters:

"To everything there is a season, and a time to every purpose under the heaven."
— Ecclesiastes 3:1

A **season** is a set or appointed time for something. **Purpose** means *delight, desire, will, pursuit,* and *matter.* Since we are located under heaven, our time here on earth is limited by the very nature of living and dying as well as the continual changing of seasons. Just like the earth itself moves with purpose our own movement must fulfill a purpose as well.

We are made aware of the proper time to move later in the same chapter:

"A time to weep, and a time to laugh; a time to mourn, and a time to dance."
– Ecclesiastes 3:4

The list of contrasts in Ecclesiastes 3 are very revealing. Time is something useful on earth, but not in heaven. Weeping, laughter and mourning are normal human expressions. These are usually exhibited as a result of some external influence.

Weeping is a response to grief through tearful expression. Laughter is related to good times in the context of playful celebration. One definition for the Hebrew use of the word **sachaq** defines laughter as *to* *play* (including instrumental music, singing, and dancing).[10]

Mourning is slightly different than weeping. Gesenuis' Hebrew Lexicon defines it (**caphad**) as *to beat the breast, as a sign of grief.* This is a type of movement!

The word used for dance in Ecclesiastes 3 is **raqad**, meaning *to skip about, to dance, to leap, to make to skip.* Not only is this type of movement radically different than beating on the breast in grief, it compels others to become joyfully physical instead.

The opposite of weeping and mourning is laughter and dance. Lamentations 5:15 further confirms this fact:

"The joy of our heart is ceased; our dance is turned into mourning."

Those who may have given up on the desire to dance may be mourning over something that has been lost. This is not exclusive to loved ones.

What you once loved and shared an intense passion for in the Lord may not be a

---

[10]

https://www.biblestudytools.com/lexicons/hebrew/nas/sachaq.html

change of season but a sense of despair. The mourning identified in this verse is the lament for that which is dead. Has something expired that is causing you grief and robbing you of the ability to express yourself through movement? There **is** a time to mourn and not dance.

Those who move through the earth with the gospel message must be able to accurately discern the times for appropriate expression. It is not always proper to just get up and dance. Our emotions can affect our outward motions. When we move outside of God's timing and purpose, we are bound to misstep.

Chapter 11

SATYRS

Christian dance proponents often focus on the obvious Scriptures concerning dance and movement. The inclination to move transcends culture, geography, and gender. Even small children respond rhythmically to music without any formal training.

The spiritual realm is not excluded from movement. Even though there are several instances of ungodly dancing in the Bible, this little-known secret reveals what we must caution against in order to separate the holy from the profane:

> **"But wild beasts of the desert shall lie there; and their houses shall be full of doleful creatures; and owls shall dwell there, and satyrs shall dance there."**
> – Isaiah 13:21

Satyr is translated from the Hebrew as a *hairy goat*, but this word is also translated as "devil."

Note that the distinction between God's people and those who are not is realized in the comparison between sheep and goats. As characteristic of the children of Israel, the tradition of worshiping idolatrous goats continued as described here:

"And they shall no more offer their sacrifices unto devils, after whom they have gone a whoring. This shall be a statute forever unto them throughout their generations."
— Leviticus 17:7

The exact same Hebrew word for satyr used in Isaiah appears here as the word devils! **Sa'iyr** is the original word that defines both instances. Many cultural traditions that involved sacrifices also incorporated dance as a form of worship or expression.

In Greek mythology, a satyr is described as a sylvan god with the appearance of a horse or goat that enjoyed extravagance.[11] Some synonyms for satyr include: *Lothario, philanderer, Don Juan, wolf,* and *womanizer.* A lothario is a man who focuses on seducing women. Philanderers are those who are

---

[11] https://mythology.net/greek/greek-creatures/satyr/

unfaithful to their wives. The traditional role of a "Don Juan" is a man who involves himself with many women. A womanizer is a man who has short, sexual relationships with many women. Do you see the pattern here?

Webster's Dictionary defines satyrs as goat-like men who drank, danced, and chased after nymphs. It also describes them as men with strong sexual desires. Many nightclubs feature this type of untamed spirit running loose to the sounds of hypnotic music, gyrating openly on the dance floor.

Although mainly descriptive of men, these characteristics are also seen in many women who joyfully embrace these types of occasions. Satyriasis is a diagnosis given to one identified as a satyr.[12] This would be a condition of a man unable to control his sexual desire. Today, this person would be referred to as a sex addict.

There are entire sects and secret societies that use dance and movement as part of ritualistic worship. This is not a new idea or

---

[12]

https://www.collinsdictionary.com/us/dictionary/english/satyriasis

tradition as we find an example of this devilish practice:

"And he ordained him priests for the high places, and for the devils, and for the calves which he had made."
— 2 Chronicles 11:15

There was always someone in leadership who desired to challenge the Almighty God by establishing an alternate worship system of their own. We must be careful that we are not introducing practices that serve our own purposes and are outside of God's instruction.

Man-made traditions have crept into the church for centuries. Several of them are still widely embraced and can be resistant to change. As the arts are being revived, some of the same dangers can obtain a foothold if we are not vigilant against them.

This type of behavior can be seen in cults. The focus is removed from God, and an alternative way of viewing Scripture or a radical redefinition of worship creeps in. These idols can take several forms. If we are not committed to the true study of God's Word, our own ministries, garments, music, cultural and denominational traditions, and even the dances themselves can become a false type of god in our lives. We must be willing to lay it all on His true altar!

Zealous ambition can also lead to a demise. The following passage describes Alexander the Great:

> **"And the rough goat is the king of Grecia: and the great horn that is between his eyes is the first king. Now that being broken, whereas four stood up for it, four kingdoms shall stand up out of the nation, but not in his power."**
>
> – Daniel 8:21-22

Alexander the Great was famous for being an ambitious military leader who welcomed danger in the face of conquering territory. In his quest for worldwide dominance, he died at the age of 33 due to sickness. Although his years were short, he made a name for himself and had an impact on history.[13]

---

[13] https://www.historyextra.com/period/ancient-greece/facts-alexander-great-life-death/

Jesus also died at the age of 33, but He was a King who gained global reign! Jesus did not fight wars through the power of human weaponry, but through the sword of the Word! His ambition was not rooted in a personal need to see His own desires fulfilled, but to do the will of His Father. He would forever change history and be honored throughout eternity.

Alexander was depicted as a rough goat. His death signaled the end of his conquests. Jesus is often described as both a Lion and a Lamb. His crucifixion facilitated His reign throughout the earth! Becoming established by earthly leadership without being purposed by God is a dangerous road to walk.

The root of our desire to dance must not be found in the appeasement of our flesh. In today's culture, dance is celebrated for the lines of the body, mastery of skill, creativity, and diversity of expression. If we veer away from implementing the Bible as our standard, we can easily slip into the enemy's trap.

How do we know if we have invented our own formula for worship? Let's examine our approach and thoughts. Do we insist that everyone embrace the same movements? Are we promoting only one style of music as acceptable? Have we instituted a set of rules that cannot be found in Scripture? Are we disassociating from those who claim Christ but don't share our same customs or educational backgrounds? Let's avoid making idols of our own imaginations, whatever the reasoning.

The Bible Dictionary depicts this sinister being as a hairy, half-goat, half-man image that inhabits desolate territories. The concept is that there is no one able to govern these behaviors in a "wild" setting that is both spiritually and naturally dry, and largely uninhabited.

Dancers in ministry cannot become so fixated on the results that we neglect the responsibilities. When the devil is granted access to our operations, we can unwittingly embrace anarchy and decline the order of God. Leaping and bucking to the beat while neglecting the incorporation of the Word is extending an invitation for the adversary to wreak havoc. Our steps must be ordered.

Those involved in the worship arts must be aware of an underlying temptation to be unfaithful to God and His covenant. Dancing David was a hero and a man after God's own heart, but he sinned when he decided to involve himself with another man's wife. Ultimately, the dancing satyr is one who adopts an ungodly lifestyle, choosing the pleasures of the flesh over the purposes of God. Let us choose life by moving according to the Word of the Lord.

Chapter 12

VIRGINS

The Lord seeks an offering of purity. Even with the dances of the children of Israel and women from all of the cities, God wanted to assure that worship was exclusive to Him. Because of the persistence of idolatry, the descendants of Israel found themselves in cycles of captivity and destruction for turning from the Lord to false gods.

The plan for redemption is revealed in Jeremiah 31:4:

"Again I will build thee, and thou shalt be built, O virgin of Israel: thou shalt again be adorned with thy tabrets, and shalt go forth in the dances of them that make merry."

God's people are given another chance to dance! He is calling forth the remnant of those who are pure and undefiled to be restored to a place of freedom in Him.

The revelation that this has to happen in a future time lets us know that Israel had been stripped of the dance and was in a state of disrepair. The prophet Jeremiah is letting the people know that tambourines and dancing will be an appropriate response to the restoration that is to come, even Christ's birth through a virgin named Mary.

Of them that make merry refers to dances performed through both instrumental and vocal methods.[14] It also means *to laugh*, meaning that the dancers will enjoy the experience as it is happening. Dance unto the Lord should be a joyous occasion!

We face a real challenge when the ministry of movement is designated as an extracurricular activity or a place where parents force their children to participate without having knowledge of God. There must be an emotional, expressed connection to the movement.

Jeremiah continues to detail the transformation that is to come in Jeremiah 31:12-13:

---

[14]https://www.blueletterbible.org/lang/Lexicon/Lexicon.cfm?strongs=H7832&t=KJV

"Therefore they shall come and sing in the height of Zion, and shall flow together to the goodness of the LORD, for wheat, and for wine, and for oil, and for the young of the flock and of the herd: and their soul shall be as a watered garden; and they shall not sorrow any more at all. Then shall the virgin rejoice in the dance, both young men and old together: for I will turn their mourning into joy, and will comfort them, and make them rejoice from their sorrow."

He is saying that they will come to Zion with joyful sounds of shouting. The journey will lead them to a higher place than where they started. The unity of purpose will allow these dancers to flow together and shine or give corporate praise as a testament to God's goodness as the Provider.

It is important for teams of dancers to maintain the bond of unity in the ministry. The purpose must be clearly identified and understood. The removal of their sorrow will be accomplished as they move together.

As the Lord meets the needs of the larger group, individual circumstances will be healed as well. Even those with personal challenges in the ministry must recognize the need to lay down solitary burdens and take up celebration for God's glory as a whole.

Not only will the pure dance, but those who surround them will be compelled to join in. As the tradition mandated men and women to dance separately, Jeremiah gives us a glimpse of a future movement that embraces both genders and the elder generation to participate at the same time.

The youth, or young warriors, rejoice in victory along with the mature men. The men in this passage are men of authority, joining in with the younger generation in giving God praise. Regardless of position or place in the community, Jeremiah foresaw a time coming when societal titles would be abandoned in preference to pure praise offered before the Lord by all.

The Lord speaks of turning their mourning into dancing, essentially becoming the Chief Choreographer on the scene! God promises to transform them, provide comfort, and exchange their sadness for joy. This is the ultimate benefit of dancing for God as opposed to dancing before the idols of this world. Dance that excludes God only results in an exhibit of the flesh, but movement directed toward the Lord changes lives and heals the emotions. In His presence is fullness of joy!

Solomon writes of witnessing a powerful demonstration in action:

"Thou art beautiful, O my love, as Tirzah, comely as Jerusalem, terrible as an army with banners."
– Song of Solomon 6:4

Solomon is describing his virginal lover in relation to an army lifting banners. She captures his attention in such a way that is larger than the influence of one person. He sees her as a standard of beauty and a representative of the kingdom as troops who bore the standard and flags in a territory. An army carrying banners would be a fearful sight because of the authority that they represented.

Solomon continues to speak of her descriptively and denotes her rarity:

"My dove, my undefiled is but one; she is the only one of her mother, she is the choice one of her that bare her. The daughters saw her, and blessed

her; yea, the queens and the concubines, and they praised her."
— Song of Solomon 6:9

She is described as a virgin, morally pure and gentle. An only child, she is treasured by her mother and celebrated by those around her. When other women saw this virgin, they spoke of her happiness. She had influence with women of high position and those who were not. Not only did the women speak well of her personally, they also discussed her among other women.

Those in the ministry of dance should be encouraged to cultivate a good reputation. Operating through pure motives, exhibiting good conduct, and maintaining integrity will bring promotion that will be more effective than any dance routine.

He again described her as an army with banners in verse 10, and then highlights her as a dance company in Song of Solomon 6:13:

"Return, return, O Shulamite; return, return, that we may look upon thee. What will ye see in the Shulamite? As it were the company of two armies."

Shulamite means *peaceful* or *perfect*. The word for company here is the Hebrew word **mechowlah**, meaning *dance*!

He describes her not as one, but as two armies dancing victoriously! This includes those who served as soldiers, as well as a general encampment or tribe of people. One woman represented an entire group. Even in dance ministries, a single person's behavior or lifestyle will serve as a representation of the entire group.

Just like these virgins of the Bible, the dancer's approach to ministry must be pure and spotless. We must hold our conduct to the standard of true believers who are not walking contrary to the message displayed through movement. The Lord is willing to bring restoration to those who may have strayed from His steps. As we go forth in dance, we must be a people pure in heart, demonstrating His full power with authority.

Chapter 13

HERODIAS' DAUGHTER

One of the most infamous accounts of dance in the Bible can be accredited to Herodias' daughter. Although the Scriptures do not mention her by name, several historical accounts identify her as Salome.[15] Instead of focusing on her name, I will look at her reference as evidence of her character.

When David danced before the Lord, it was recorded that Michal, Saul's daughter, looked at him from the window. Although she was actually David's wife, her response was more like her father's. David being celebrated by the dancing women caused Saul to view David with an envious eye from that moment forward.

Miriam can be identified in a similar fashion. As Miriam placed the timbrel in her

---

[15] https://www.britannica.com/biography/Salome-stepdaughter-of-Herod-Antipas

135

hand, she is described as being "the sister of Aaron," and not the sibling of Moses, even though she was his sister as well. After Moses left Aaron in charge, the people wildly danced around a golden calf. Though Miriam led all of the women in movement, her criticism of Moses caused her to be placed outside of the camp for seven days. Both Miriam and Aaron's actions as leaders had an adverse effect on the children of Israel.

The most infamous account of dance in the Bible involves the daughter of Herodias, who danced at Herod's birthday in Matthew 14:6-9:

"But when Herod's birthday was kept, the daughter of Herodias danced before them, and pleased Herod. Whereupon he promised with an oath to give her whatsoever she would ask. And she, being before instructed of her mother, said, Give me here John Baptist's head in a charger. And the king was sorry: nevertheless for the oath's sake, and them which sat with him at meat, he commanded it to be given her."

Herod Antipas, name meaning "heroic," had placed John the Baptist in prison because of Herodias. (Ironically, her name also means "heroic" as the female equivalent to Herod). Herod was a common name of a family of male rulers. He was in a romantic relationship with his brother Phillip's wife Herodias and John the Baptist spoke out against it.

Because John the Baptist was respected as a prophet among the people, a fearful Herod Antipas opted to lock him in prison instead of taking his life. John the Baptist must have had access to this ruler in order to tell him that having a relationship with Phillip's wife was illegal. Herod chose to silence the prophet by removing him from his presence.

It is ironic that the same Greek word used in the Scripture here for birthday (**genesia**) means both a celebration and a festival to commemorate the dead (used by early Greeks).[16] Herodias took center stage, dancing in such a way that Herod's favor

---

[16]

https://www.blueletterbible.org/lang/Lexicon/Lexicon.cfm?strongs=G1077&t=KJV

was obtained to make a life-altering request. Notice that the text says she "danced before them," indicating that a viewing audience was present!

Although the Greek word used for dance here (**orcheomai**) is a generic definition, its impact was magnanimous. Herod made a sudden promise to grant his lover's daughter whatever she requested. Since kings were bound to honor any verbal or contractual agreements made, Herodias cunningly trained her daughter to ask for a sinister desire: The head of John the Baptist on a platter. Herod could not retract the promise he made, and so the prophetic voice was extinguished because of a dance.

Another account of this tragic moment is found in Mark 6:17-28:

"For Herod himself had sent forth and laid hold upon John, and bound him in prison for Herodias' sake, his brother Philip's wife: for he had married her. For John had said unto Herod, It is not lawful for thee to have thy brother's wife. Therefore Herodias had a quarrel against him, and would have killed him; but she could not: For Herod feared John, knowing that he was a

just man and an holy, and observed him; and when he heard him, he did many things, and heard him gladly. And when a convenient day was come, that Herod on his birthday made a supper to his lords, high captains, and chief estates of Galilee; And when the daughter of the said Herodias came in, and danced, and pleased Herod and them that sat with him, the king said unto the damsel, Ask of me whatsoever thou wilt, and I will give it thee. And he sware unto her, Whatsoever thou shalt ask of me, I will give it thee, unto the half of my kingdom. And she went forth, and said unto her mother, What shall I ask? And she said, The head of John the Baptist. And she came in straightway with haste unto the king, and asked, saying, I will that thou give me by and by in a charger the head of John the Baptist. And the king was exceeding sorry; yet for his oath's sake, and for their sakes which sat with him, he would not reject her. And immediately the king sent an executioner, and commanded his head to be brought: and he went and beheaded him in the prison, And brought his head in a charger, and gave it to the damsel: and the damsel gave it to her mother."

This was the dance of a mercenary. As a crafty puppet master, Herodias employed her daughter to complete the mission that she herself was unable to perform. Herod was willing to retain the company of Herodias by any means necessary. Although he listened to John the Baptist, Herod was manipulated into removing the prophetic protection in order to please her.

He also wanted to impress those who were celebrating with him at the birthday feast. As a wealthy ruler, he enticed her with a potential fortune for performing such a pleasing number. He became immediately aware of the trick as soon as her request was made.

Some would use this example as a reason to justify why dance has no place in worship today. The real truth is that dance has been an essential component in the lives and expressions of God's people for ages. It is the misuse of what was created for God's glory that will hinder the Word of the Lord from being heard.

For worship artists today, it is important that parents refrain from manipulating their children to dance for reasons that are not exclusive to pleasing the Lord. Family members should not seek to encourage children and teens to dance for ungodly gain or to satisfy selfish personal needs for applause or emotional feelings of pride when they go forth in dance.

Likewise, adults should not use the art of dance merely to obtain fame, money, status, or a position. When we do so, we silence the voice of God in our lives. Dance can serve as a weapon anytime hidden motives are present.

Chapter 14

THE PRODIGAL SON'S COMMUNITY

I have heard the story of the prodigal son preached countless times. Until I decided to study movement in the Scriptures, I had no idea that dance was a part of this celebration because it was skipped over. We won't miss this moment of revelation.

I heard about how the younger son wanted his inheritance. I was warned of his foolish choices as he wasted his substance on riotous living. I was reminded that he returned home after he shared a meal with the pigs. I know that his father welcomed him home with open arms.

His father did not simply say, "Welcome home!" He instructed his servants to bring jewelry, clothing and shoes. Whenever a ruler wanted to honor someone, he would do so with a necklace or a ring and luxurious clothing. The prodigal son received honor from his father when most people would have disqualified him.

His older brother was not amused by the joyful scene. Luke 15:20-82 depicts his epic disappointment.

"And he arose, and came to his father. But when he was yet a great way off, his father saw him, and had compassion, and ran, and fell on his neck, and kissed him. And the son said unto him, Father, I have sinned against heaven, and in thy sight, and am no more worthy to be called thy son. But the father said to his servants, Bring forth the best robe, and put it on him; and put a ring on his hand, and shoes on his feet: And bring hither the fatted calf, and kill it; and let us eat, and be merry: For this my son was dead, and is alive again; he was lost, and is found. And they began to be merry. Now his elder son was in the field: and as he came and drew nigh to the house, he heard musick and dancing. And he called one of the servants, and asked what these things meant. And he said unto him, Thy brother is come; and thy father hath killed the fatted calf, because he hath received him safe and

sound. And he was angry, and would not go in: therefore came his father out, and intreated him."

There are several amazing points for us to note from Luke Chapter 15. The son rehearsed what he would say to his father before he stood in his presence (Luke 15:18-19). When he finally made it, he did not get to get to the part he rehearsed to say, "Make me as one of the hired servants." Just because he sinned did not mean that he had lost the relationship with his father. There will be times that we will rehearse what we have planned, but the Father will interrupt with a much better one.

The father showed affection to his son before verbal repentance was offered. How many times have we heard stories about people coming to church and being mistreated or judged instead of shown compassion? There may be those that leave the group and then return to the dance ministry. When they do, we should receive them with compassion.

The prodigal son realized the error of his ways. Too many people enter into a back-slidden condition and expect to return to service with no questions asked. Both his words and his actions showed that he had experienced a change of heart. Notice that his father did not respond with an "I told you so" response. He instructed his servants to provide the items that would represent the son's restoration.

The servants also had to serve the son by placing the ring, shoes, and robe on him. When people return after experiencing a setback, they may need some help from those who serve in the Father's house. We must be willing to serve where there is a need as well as a command to do so.

"And they began to be merry..." An act of repentance was an occasion for great gladness. The celebration was not limited to the father and his son. The musicians and the dancers were present! Instead of punishing the younger son for his misdeeds, the return to his father's house was cause for a party! When a brother or sister wanders away and comes back home, it is a perfect time to get the music going and dance!

There are several occasions in the Old Testament that show the marriage between music and movement. This reinforces the concept of the worship arts units working in conjunction at public gatherings. There is a natural correlation between music and the need to respond to it physically.

What happens behind the scenes can also provide valuable lessons for us. The older son was in the field, which probably meant that he was working hard with what produced the wealth in the first place. As he returned home from work, he was horrified to know that a celebration was being held without his consent. He did not immediately enter the house, but asked one of the servants what was happening.

He did not take the news well at all! *How could they celebrate his younger brother who had abandoned the family while he stayed home and remained faithful?* He was working in the field while they danced to the music. *How was this justice?*

He refused to enter his father's presence because of the anger he had toward his brother. There may be some of us right now who refuse to enter the church building because there are some unresolved issues that we are too angry to confront directly. His father had to come to the place where he communicated with the older brother. Whether faithful or not, none of us are uninvited from the dance.

The word used for dancing here is the Greek word *choros*, which means a band (of dancers and singers), circular dance, a dance, dancing.[17] They sung their hearts out. They danced around the room. They were playing while the elder son was working. Did his father forget that his brother had brought shame to the family name?

The elder son felt that his loyalty should have resulted in something worth far more than his brother could receive for mishandling his father's funds. He approached the house and heard the music and rhythmic movements from within. He probably had to double-check to make sure that he was not imagining things.

How did the servant know so much about what was happening in his father's presence and he knew nothing? He protested. Since he felt excluded, he decided to stay

---

[17]

https://www.blueletterbible.org/lang/Lexicon/Lexicon.cfm?strongs=G5525&t=KJV

out. His father never threw him a party! *Was this the thanks he got?*

Recognizing his son's deep discouragement, the father explained that all that he possessed was already his. The elder son's propensity for self-righteousness prevented him from seeing that his little brother needed restoration. If we are honest, many of us can relate to this story.

Becoming a worship artist is relatively easy. When people fail in what we call the secular world, they may decide to return to the congregation to gain a new opportunity. Some who have been faithful in serving may feel that it is unfair for a celebrity to receive an immediate promotion, or for someone who was backslidden to return to a position of ministry. Our Father reminds us to welcome them and to dance for joy when they make it back home.

Chapter 15

ME

I had no idea that I would end up serving in the ministry of movement as a minister, leader, and speaker for over 15 years when I first started. At the age of 15, I wrote a play entitled, "The Perfect Sacrifice." In it, I included two dancing angels. Over 25 years ago, I had no desire to actually dance myself. Although I was always on the drill team or was a cheerleader in school, my dream job was to be a casting director.

We completed the play and I moved on to my next creative venture. Three years later at the age of 18, I was confronted with the option to worship the Lord beyond my personal comfort zone.

Though I am naturally expressive, I was not the type of young person who lifted my hands to the Lord beyond the mandatory movements included in a few of our youth choir songs. While seated and waiting for us to be called to the choir stand, I seldom considered praising the Lord outside of our group's turn to sing.

As a young adult, I joined the Los Angeles Cathedral Choir in 1994 and attended a scheduled event. As destiny would have it, there was a praise dance ministry on program. I sat in that church and watched a group called "The Hush Company" dance to "I Know I've Been Changed" by LaShun Pace. It was then that I knew that there was more to worship than singing in the choir or from the congregation.

Those young people moved with such force and conviction! I thought that my natural reaction would have been to shout "Hallelujah" and stand up and sway. I sat there staring. Stunned. *Was this actually possible?* Suddenly, I felt the urge to dance for the Lord. It would have to wait a few years.

At the age of 21, I approached my new church with another drama production. I included dancers once again, but this time, I would be the lead choreographer. Seven dancers signed up, and we began rehearsing in my living room.

The first question that church leadership asked us was, "What are you going to wear?" Since we were in a Church of God in Christ congregation, we understood the importance of being properly dressed for worship. We made sure that our under-garments and outer garments were beyond reproach. Resurrection Sunday came, and we danced our hearts out.

I was elated! The church was blessed and I found a way to honor God that included my love for music, dance, and drama all in one! I asked the group of girls if they wanted to continue. Of the initial seven, only two of us decided to pursue this new avenue.

When I approached my church with our excitement, they told me to go talk to the leader of the Teen Ministry. Being in my twenties, that made absolutely no sense to me. With our pastor's blessing, we began an independent ministry that would not be a part of the church, but was accountable to its leadership.

While standing in the hallway of my apartment, I heard the Spirit of the Lord tell me, "Envision Worship Dancers." I called my partner and told her our new name! She loved it. We commissioned a custom made emerald green dance garment, ordered business cards, and we were on our way!

Our first ministry engagement was for a women's event. From there, it seemed that we were constantly booked. At one point, it felt like we were dancing every Friday, Saturday, and Sunday, and sometimes more than once in a day! The excitement and affirmation of seeing people set free by dance almost became an addiction. I soon learned the danger of making a ministry an idol.

During my time in Envision, I became engaged. My fiancé was a professional musician and landed a gig with a legendary artist shortly after we began dating. He had to relocate to Las Vegas, Nevada to work with the artist while I kept my residence in Long Beach, California. We kept up with our wedding plans and got married in 2002.

I did not move immediately. After all, we did not know how long the artist would continue to perform in Las Vegas. I had a great job in my native Southern California comfort zone. Life was good.

We would either fly or drive to see each other every single weekend. I did not have much time to be distracted because the dance ministry was so popular. We even hosted our very first dance conference in 2003, entitled "Rain." Because of the unusual move of God that would take place when we danced, I was convinced that the Lord would not have me give up the duet just yet.

We would receive prophecies that we would travel around the world with dance ministry. It had not yet happened, so I had to hold on. We stayed active, ministering throughout Southern California, but seldom ventured beyond that.

Eventually, we began to grow apart. Although I was aware that things were changing between us, I was still convinced that I had to hold on to the ministry. It got to the point that we were having major disagreements and discord began to unravel our tight bond.

I was at a crossroads! My dance partner was my best friend. Not only that, we looked so much alike that people thought we were twins, or at least sisters. I finally arrived at the place where the Lord told me to release the ministry. I grieved over the decision.

I called my closest friends to come and witness our final evening of ministry as Envision. Some of them questioned my judgment and said that they were not sure that I had heard from God. I had no doubt that I received instructions and had no choice but to obey Him.

As I waited for our name to be called, it felt as though every song that we had ever danced to was sung by the host choir or referenced by the emcee. My partner and I barely spoke any words to each other while we waited. I shifted in my seat. She laughed nervously. They called us up for the grand finale.

I had to move before the congregation in a broken state. How can you partner with someone on the dance floor and barely interact with them? We made it through the piece and service ended. I was shaking as my feet headed in her direction. I grabbed her by the hands, thanked her for being my partner over the years, and ended the ministry. Just. Like. That.

Somehow, I expected it to end peacefully, but it was dramatic. Thankfully, most of the audience was gone and only our friends remained. After the "break-up," I got into my car, pulled out my towel, and broke down in tears.

It was as if I had to place my most beloved possession into a fire. I had neglected my spouse, endured persecution, and spent lots of money on the ministry. Had it all been worth it?

Although our ministry was over, we had not yet terminated the strife. We were still members of the same church. Once seated together, we were now on different rows. The tension was almost unbearable. Other people in our congregation began to take sides and ask awkward questions. We still had a hard time speaking to each other.

I served as the dance leader at our church, although Envision was always a separate group. I figured that maybe my time to dance had ended, and I would just enjoy choreographing for the girls. I was wrong.

I received a call from our pastor, asking me to dance solo at his appreciation service.

What? Immediately, I said "No!" I caught myself for a moment and began to explain to him why that could not be done. "What are people going to say?" "She is going to be there! I do not want to hurt her!" He calmly replied, "You should dance because I asked you to." I was speechless.

I guess it was going to be just me and Jesus. I purchased bright yellow material, took it to the tailor, selected a song, and a new chapter in my life began. With the support of my husband, friends and supporters, I stepped out on faith.

I was nervous! I knew without a doubt that we were anointed as Envision, but how would Rekesha Pittman compare? When choreographing as a duo, team, or a group, I would receive immediate feedback as to what was working or needed adjustment. Alone, all I had was a mirror and a hope that the dance would be effective.

The big day came and the church was packed. I sat on the end of the pew at the edge of my seat. They called my name and I felt like all eyes were watching me. The music started and "Endow Me" by Twinkie Clark resonated throughout the room. I moved with all of the power I had within me. Tears flowed. Hands were lifted. The last few seconds of the song brought great elation to my spirit. Whew! It was over and I made it through.

The battle was not yet over. The division between my former partner and I had reached an unbearable state. We scheduled a meeting with our church leaders. More tears. No resolution. To make things worse, the dancers that I led at our church began to openly challenge my leadership. It was all too much.

My husband and I made a decision to move on. We could no longer knowingly support division within our congregation. We informed our pastor, said farewell to friends, and departed. It hurt.

It seemed as though my obedience to God caused my world to fall apart. We decided to attend a church where we could be restored without having to serve in ministry. It was all a set-up from on High!

The weekly commute between California and Nevada was no longer a necessity. One night, my husband called while driving from Las Vegas to Long Beach. He said, "I'm so sleepy." All I could imagine was getting a call that my man had crashed into the side of a mountain, trying to maintain a reality that was no longer sustainable for us. I gave my job a two-month notice and started the process that would uproot my life as a California native to become a resident of "Sin City."

Like most people who go to Las Vegas, I had a fantasy of how easy life would be if I made the right moves at the right time. I packed up my residence in Long Beach. He drove the moving truck and I drove for five hours into Nevada, my car overloaded by the weight of my belongings. Having never lived outside of California, it was a major life-decision for me.

Since my husband was already employed in the entertainment industry in Las Vegas, we were able to secure a condo before my arrival. I thought that I would be happy living in that beautiful city, but as I looked around, I immediately began to miss the oceanfront living and cooler weather that I had become accustomed to.

Ironically, because I was still known for dance ministry all over Southern California,

I drove back to the Los Angeles area at least twice monthly on assignment. Most of the time, those who invited me did not realize that I had already moved out of state. I can attribute that to the fact that I did not tell them.

As God really began to speak to me about my role in the dance ministry in Nevada, I was overwhelmed with feelings of inadequacy. I did not have a network of people to contact. My track record was in California. I had no idea where to start.

I performed a general internet search on "Praise Dance in Las Vegas," and very few names appeared. The main one that stood out was "Ms. Michelle," who was listed as the dance leader of Mountaintop Faith Ministries at that time.

I visited a few local churches to survey the dance ministry scene. I asked questions about how the dance community interacted and was told that very little collaboration took place. I still journeyed to Los Angeles to get my ministry "fix." That was until the Lord told me, "I need you to stop going to California every month and grow roots in Las Vegas."

A short while after (and to my surprise), I got a personal phone call from "Ms. Michelle" herself! She invited me to minister at an upcoming praise dance concert that was going to be held at the West Las Vegas Library Theater. She humorously informed me that she had heard some things about me. Apparently, the rumor in the church community was that I thought that I was going to take over praise dance. She said if that many people had something to say about me, she knew that I must be somebody she had to invite. I was amused as well.

After accepting her invitation, my mind began to wander. *Who in the world would spread such gossip about me?* I decided to let it go and prepared for the gathering.

I chose to present one of my signature pieces, "When the Saints Go to Worship," by Benita Washington. Although Donald Lawrence and the Tri-City Singers had already recorded a more popular version of the song, Benita's version resonated with me deeply.

I pulled up to the theater, car loaded with a golden treasure chest, a folding chair, and a brocade jacket dance garment. I was a bit nervous, but decided to focus on the worship experience. Always the one to stand out, this time was no different.

After I got dressed, one of the dance leaders remarked, "I like your dress. I would buy garments like that but my team cannot afford it." I almost laughed out loud! Because I had a great relationship with my seamstress, I purchased the fabric and only paid $40.00 for the actual sewing work!

I was up to dance next. The music started and I began to worship the Lord through movement. After I left the stage, dancers were backstage with their hands lifted or were kneeling over in tears. The audience kept praising... and shouting... and praising... and shouting. The concert came to a complete standstill.

One dancer ran up to me and grabbed me around my neck. She said, "I don't know who you are, but that blessed me!" I could only honor God for His visitation that night.

I was led to launch the Las Vegas Liturgical Dance Network in 2006. I visited a local library, secured a community meeting room and spread the word. Many dance ministry leaders were in attendance and let me know that an effort to bring the liturgical dance community had taken place before, but it had been a while since there was unity in the community.

One of the problems that I encountered came from one of the leaders who apparently had a different vision of what the network should be. She was very vocal in her expressiveness. It got to the point where another leader warned me about what would happen if the vision did not remain clear.

Although I had already hosted several dance conferences at the church level, I ventured into my first hotel conference in October of 2007. After advertising the conference through email, I received an irate message from a believer who questioned why I would take the saints to "Sin City" for a dance conference. I let her know that the rebuke was unwarranted as I was a resident of Las Vegas. I replied to her, "There are Christians here, too. We believe that this conference will be an amazing opportunity for evangelism."

"24/7-365: Eternal Worship" was held at the Tuscany Suites to a packed house nightly. We ended the conference with a live worship in dance experience on the world-famous Las Vegas Strip! Dance ministries in attendance danced at the Hawaiian Marketplace outdoor pavilion. The dancers filled the space and total strangers joined in the praise as they passed by.

There were people drinking alcohol and smoking while they watched. By the time the dance concert was over, several people received prayer and asked to be led to Christ. One dancer approached me with tears in her eyes and told me that she had danced in the church, but had never experienced an outreach event like that. Although I was the conference host, I was completely humbled that God would open a door of favor that would allow us to minister freely in a place known for its sin.

A conference that saved souls, shifted mindsets, and established a strong message of evangelism was followed by a strong spirit of depression. I had never faced anything like it before. Although we were able to meet our budgetary requirements, the sheer trauma and backlash of hosting an event of that magnitude was fierce!

I would lay in my bed in the dark for hours at a time in the daylight hours. Still an active member at my church, I found myself crying uncontrollably at times during the service. I just wasn't myself.

I was often asked to minister in movement for other churches and organizations. After mustering up enough strength to get dressed, drive to the location and minister with power, I would return home to my familiar prison and sink back down into my bed of darkness. People would tell me how much they were blessed by my ministry. They had no idea what level of sacrifice it took just to walk out of the door of my house.

Through all of that, I still served my community through the dance network. We entered our first Martin Luther King Jr. Parade as an organization in January of 2008. We had rehearsed for about a month before the big day.

We donned our dance garments, carried our Las Vegas Liturgical Dance Network sign, and ministered along the parade route.

Although it was 29 degrees that day, the unity displayed brought warmth to my heart!

Still, no one could bring me out of the valley of sorrow. One day, I was in bed and I heard the Lord tell me to get up and write three to four paragraphs about dance ministry each day. I launched a blog called, "Company Keepers: Dance Ministry Talk," and wrote faithfully. That spirit of depression finally broke! I wrote every day for an entire year. My first book emerged.

Since the time I relocated to Las Vegas, I prayed for years to the Lord about starting a professional Christian dance company in the city. In 2009, I heard the Lord tell me that the time was right to start. I purchased a domain name for the website, obtained a business license, headed down to my local radio station to book a commercial, and Reign Dance Company was born!

I scheduled Sunday ads on the radio to target the faith-based community. To my dismay, the telephone number that they gave on the air was incorrect! The Lord has a way of working things out, nevertheless. The radio station agreed to re-record my ad and ran the spot during the weekdays in prime radio slots! The phone began ringing and the rest, as they say, was history!

Instead of hosting company auditions, I held an open house enrollment for dancers ages 10 and up. I did not want anyone to feel rejected. We strongly encouraged adults to enroll.

We ended up with 11 committed dancers and began formal training. Less than one month after we opened, we got a call to dance with Gospel singer Chris Bolton for a concert that he was having in Las Vegas. We contacted a local seamstress, ordered 11 red dance overlays, and our public debut was set! We ministered to "Let the Praise Begin" (the version by Fred Hammond). Reign Dance Company (RDC) continued to minister throughout the city over the next several years almost nonstop.

As an established leader in the worship arts in Southern California, I held annual dance conferences since 2003. After moving to Las Vegas, due to the expense of hosting events there, I decided to host them every two years instead of yearly.

RDC was invited to participate at my "Dance Ministry Detox" conference in 2009 in Las Vegas. Again, we hosted a capacity crowd and RDC ministered on a national platform for the first time.

Our popularity continued to soar. We were frequently requested for several major citywide events including a gospel fest for our local radio station, women's conferences, themed programs, church banquets, private weddings, anniversaries, and special celebrations. The years just seemed to fly by!

Just one year after our launch, we hosted our first dance production, "A Night in Shining Armor." By that time, the company had grown to 23 dancers. We booked the Flamingo Library Theater and sold nearly 300 tickets. There were even two separate groups that traveled from California to dance in the lineup.

We also ventured out of state to several dance conferences and productions including St. Louis, MO; Long Beach, CA; Los Angeles, CA; Compton, CA; and Tampa, FL.

2011 would change the trajectory of our company forever! I was invited to speak at an event in June. Near the end of the service, a prophet got up and told us that we were going to go to South Africa. We were excited to hear the news and looked forward to God moving on our behalf in the future. That moment was much closer than we realized.

Three weeks later, I was a guest speaker at a conference in Georgia. On the last day of the gathering, a man approached me and said, "I am Minister Neville from South Africa. We would like to invite you and your team to South Africa." I was stunned. First of all, my team did not go to Georgia with me, so how did he know that I had a team? Secondly, we had just heard this prophecy. It all felt very sudden.

I hosted a conference called "Worship, Incorporated" in August of that same year. We raised money for South Africa by allowing our members to set up booths at the conference. The support was mind-blowing!

We hit the Las Vegas Strip once again to dance as a form of evangelism at the end of the gathering. It was one of the most intense worship experiences that I have had the privilege of attending. I distinctly remember one lady worshiping on her face on the concrete sidewalk at the end of the night.

As the favor of the Lord would have it, we were in South Africa three months later. Seven of us, plus two guides, ministered in Soweto, Johannesburg, Pretoria, and Cape Town over the course of 12 days. I took several copies of my books, which were two at that time, and blessed dance ministers with them. That experience shaped my focus as a Worship Arts Missionary going forward.

I learned from South Africa that I had to do more than just speak at workshops. If I was going to make a difference, I had to "sow" into that land to leave a legacy beyond my presence. I decided from then on to take garments, books, billows, flags, and any other items that would be a blessing if we expected the dancers to retain and implement what we instructed.

I soon learned that I did not have to go to another nation to leave a legacy. We were invited to minister at the Chino Women's Correctional Facility for female inmates. To our surprise, the prison had a dance ministry called "Hyssop." It consisted of 17 dancers. We thought that we were going to bless them, but they asked to pray for us! We exchanged dances and encouragement. The warden granted me permission to sign 17 copies of my very first book, "Company Keepers: Dance Ministry Daily," and each member of Hyssop received a signed copy to keep with them.

Beyond the many highlights and memorable moments, the lives that have been touched through dance ministry for me has changed my life forever. I have had my share of dark days as well. There have been numerous times when I had no desire to dance. To support my apathy, I would often gorge on food to give myself an excuse for why I could not fit my garments or was too out-of-shape to rehearse or move.

I then realized that the Lord was shifting me into another area of ministry. Through my love for dance, I developed a strong habit of studying God's Word. Dance Conferences allowed me to develop my teaching and preaching ministry as a guest facilitator. Writing books opened up new doors for me to train hundreds of authors to publish worldwide. Dance ministry has definitely been a vehicle that has taken me numerous places!

In 2012, I answered an additional calling and became an ordained pastor. As a bonus, I became pregnant with my first child and received my ordination with a round belly and a glowing face! As exciting as the new season was, it came with its own set of challenges.

Because I was known for dance in my local community, there were people who had a hard time accepting me as a pastor. Even though I am a respected speaker internationally, my city just wanted to see me dance. I had to embrace my calling and ignore the chatter.

Although I continued to lead my group, I had been training several others on the team to choreograph and run the operations of RDC. I would travel to preach or teach and the company would continue moving forward without my presence. We continued to support each other and traveled many places together.

The year 2013 proved to be a turning point in my life. I hosted "Dance Leaders Advance" and offered brand new classes that embraced business, technology, and innovation for arts leaders. As a bonus, I decided to write a complimentary "e-book" to give away to all of the conference attendees, but the Lord instructed me to publish it for the masses. "Dance Leaders Advance" has become one of my most popular books and workshops to date!

I am now interested in reproducing the gifts God gave me and assisting others in the activation of theirs. Since I am an author who trains authors, I asked each member of Reign Dance Company to write one chapter about their leadership role and experience in RDC. In April of 2014, we released our anthology "Training to Reign" in conjunction with our dance production entitled, "The Son and the Reign."

We took another missions trip to the Bahamas in July of 2014. This time, the entire team went! One of the highlights of the trip was when we danced at a cultural exchange for the people of the Bahamas. A short while after the concert ended, the heavens poured down rain and we practically had to swim back to our hotel!

I was compelled to make a major shift once again in 2015. I was running "The Assembling Worship Center" as a pastor, leading Reign Dance Company, mothering a young child, teaching author courses, and running my business. It started to become overwhelming.

To make matters worse, I was extremely disappointed with some of the behavior I witnessed among the higher ranks of dance ministry leadership. Where there should have been unity and cooperation, instead there was competition and comparison. I decided to officially retire from dance and movement ministry.

I made the official announcement on social media and the word spread quickly. My family relocated to Texas and I said farewell to my beloved Reign Dance Company. It was time to begin a new chapter.

Just when I thought that my contribution to the worship arts was done, the Lord instructed me to return to teach theology to dancers, churches, and organizations to help repair some of the damage and plant a burning desire in others to study and apply the Word in fresh and creative ways. This book is my "yes" to God.

I don't want the glory or the credit. It is my hope that a worship arts revival breaks out across the globe in churches, homes, schools, and communities as God's intent for the arts in the spreading of the Gospel comes into a greater level of maturity. I have mourned the state of the movement ministry long enough. Once again, it is time for me to dance!

Chapter 16

YOU

You can express your praise to the Lord through dance! Don't think that you have to have an elaborate routine, fancy garments, or the latest music. Use your entire being to demonstrate your adoration to God and take dominion over your own flesh.

I believe that we have drifted too far away from the community dance experience and embraced more of an entertainment spirit. Many modern churches have given a platform to performers instead of crafting praise and worship atmospheres that involve entire congregations.

Keeping things in perspective, there are several sectors of the charismatic church in America that regularly experience spontaneous outbreaks of radical movement. This is often referred to as "catching the Spirit." As part of my experience in Africa, cultural dance was freely embraced as a regular part of the worship service.

While not everyone chooses to sing, clap, or dance at the same time, expressive movement should be embraced by all of us as a valid and desirable offering of praise that is acceptable to God. It is up to you to refuse to be a spectator and participate with joy!

You can praise Him at home. Stand up on your feet, lift your hands, and move your body! One of the things that I observe about my own daughter is that when she is happy, she skips, laughs, and raises her hands with gleeful expressions. We should come before Him like a little child.

Don't be afraid to praise Him in the congregation. If you attend an assembly that prohibits worship expression, I pray that you get to a place where the Spirit of the Lord grants you liberty. I am not implying that you should run down to the front of the church and render a solo. When you reach a point where you are not encumbered by what other people think, you can truly focus all of your affections on Him.

Men of God move too! I am praying that men of faith are not satisfied with allowing a majority of women to step out and minister through movement without them. David was a strong, fervent dancer. We need more men with passion like him to lead entire nations in demonstrated worship!

Even if you have physical limitations that prevent you from dancing, command your body to surrender to the Lord the glory that is due Him! Pain must yield to His presence! Diseases must bow before Him! Your age is not a disqualifier when it comes to being moved with praise! Dance before the Lord! Yes, **you!**

CONCLUSION

A small word can have big implications. Dance has remained at a surface level in the church for longer than it should have. That time is no more.

Dance is not restricted to the youth and teens, nor is it only an activity reserved for women. Not all dance is holy and acceptable as worship. We have largely left decisions about the role of dance to people and leadership that have never fully studied it. Those who have accepted positions in dance ministry leadership often emphasize the movement over the message. Powerfully authentic moves of God can only be un-earthed by studying the Word.

God is our Chief Choreographer. When He did not move, no one did. We should adhere to the same mindset today.

Week after week, and on numerous programs, untrained and unknowledgeable dancers twirl and call it ministry. Without having a love for the One who directs us, how can we truly move a people into His presence?

Debates continue about proper dance ministry attire, movement protocol, appropriate choreography, and a list of multiple opinions about what is right and wrong. Without scriptural backing, our handbooks, rules, and regulations are only the mere requirements of men without the leading of God.

My prayer is that a burning desire for the Spirit of God and our absolute need to study to show ourselves approved unto Him are more important than our experiences and viewpoints. Let's stop defending our preferred practices and stand on His Word solely.

When dancers worldwide are unified in their love for the things of God, miracles, signs, and wonders will manifest through creative acts. We need more biblically-based textbooks, communities, programs, courses, institutes, and churches that insist that every facet of ministry to God is rooted in the Scriptures. This can only happen through study and the application of sound doctrine.

I don't know about you, but I have seen enough of the same thing for far too long. Let us move away from taking baby steps and leap into the fullness of God's revelation concerning the dance. Denominations, leaders, and preachers everywhere must not minimize the importance of knowing the Word of God for all believers; especially those who serve in God's name. The only true way to move in true power is to move through the Scriptures.

ARE YOU READY TO MOVE?

Moving Through the Scriptures™ is a revolutionary educational program for movement artists worldwide! Innovative training, community connectivity, and movement with a purpose.

Explore an in-depth study of biblical dance utilizing the Moving Through the Scriptures™ textbook. MTTS offers a 90-day Immersion program instructed by Rekesha Pittman. Study groups and study aids available.

Become certified as a **Moving Through the Scriptures**™ instructor! Register online:

MovingThroughTheScriptures.com

REKESHA PITTMAN

Rekesha Pittman has been graced to stand before God's congregation with unusual boldness. Her intense desire for ministerial excellence has opened doors for her to minister in both dance and teaching of the Word on a national and international level.

Rekesha serves as workshop facilitator, mentor, consultant, and intercessor for various dance ministries, churches, worship arts departments, and music ministries. Her innermost desire is that pleasing the Lord remain the focus of service in ministry, and that worship becomes an essential component in the daily life of every believer in the Body of Christ.

ADDITIONAL BOOKS BY
REKESHA PITTMAN

Company Keepers: Dance Ministry Daily

Dance Leaders Advance

For This Cause, I Bow My Knees:
A Moving Testament

Training to Reign

7 Steps to a Divine Dance Company

Get Write, Church!

ABCs of Authorship

Book Publishing Master Plan

Birth of a Saleswoman

Hire Learning

Masterful Mentorship

ORDER YOUR COPIES TODAY!

BooksbyRekesha.com

.

Made in the USA
Monee, IL
26 August 2023

41673431R00109